W9-BJU-846

WITHDRAWN
NDSU

HUMAN SHOWS
FAR PHANTASIES

THE MACMILLAN COMPANY
NEW YORK · BOSTON · CHICAGO · DALLAS
ATLANTA · SAN FRANCISCO

MACMILLAN & CO., LIMITED
LONDON · BOMBAY · CALCUTTA
MELBOURNE

THE MACMILLAN CO. OF CANADA, LTD.
TORONTO

HUMAN SHOWS FAR PHANTASIES

SONGS, AND TRIFLES

BY

THOMAS HARDY

39816

NEW YORK
THE MACMILLAN COMPANY
1925

All Rights Reserved

821
H22h

Copyright, 1925,
By THE MACMILLAN COMPANY.

Set up and electrotyped.
Published December, 1925.

PR
4750
H7
1925

Printed in the United States of America by
THE FERRIS PRINTING COMPANY, NEW YORK.

Educ.
7.68.
Macmillan
20 ja. - 26

CONTENTS

PAGE

WAITING BOTH 1
A BIRD-SCENE AT A RURAL DWELLING 2
"ANY LITTLE OLD SONG" 3
IN A FORMER RESORT AFTER MANY YEARS 4
A CATHEDRAL FAÇADE AT MIDNIGHT 5
THE TURNIP-HOER 7
THE CARRIER 13
LOVER TO MISTRESS 14
THE MONUMENT-MAKER 15
CIRCUS-RIDER TO RINGMASTER 17
LAST WEEK IN OCTOBER 19
COME NOT; YET COME! 20
THE LATER AUTUMN 21
"LET ME" 23
AT A FASHIONABLE DINNER 24
GREEN SLATES 26
AN EAST-END CURATE 27
AT RUSHY-POND 29
FOUR IN THE MORNING 31
ON THE ESPLANADE 33
IN ST. PAUL'S A WHILE AGO 35
COMING UP OXFORD STREET: EVENING 37
A LAST JOURNEY 39

39816

CONTENTS

PAGE

Singing Lovers 42
The Month's Calendar 44
A Spellbound Palace 45
When Dead 47
Sine Prole 48
Ten Years since 49
Every Artemisia 50
The best she could 52
The Graveyard of Dead Creeds 54
"There seemed a Strangeness" 56
A Night of Questionings 57
Xenophanes, the Monist of Colophon 61
Life and Death at Sunrise 64
Night-time in Mid-fall 66
A Sheep Fair 67
Snow in the Suburbs 69
A Light Snow-fall after Frost 71
Winter Night in Woodland 73
Ice on the Highway 75
Music in a Snowy Street 76
The Frozen Greenhouse 78
Two Lips 80
No Buyers 81
One who married above Him 83
The New Toy 87
Queen Caroline to her Guests 88
Plena Timoris 90
The Weary Walker 92
Last Love-word 93
Nobody comes 94
In the Street 95

PAGE

The Last Leaf 96
At Wynyard's Gap 98
At Shag's Heath 109
A Second Attempt 112
"Freed the Fret of Thinking" 114
The Absolute explains 115
"So, Time" 120
An Inquiry 121
The Faithful Swallow 123
In Sherborne Abbey 124
The Pair he saw pass 127
The Mock Wife 130
The Flight on Durnover Moor 133
Last Look round St. Martin's Fair 137
The Caricature 139
A Leader of Fashion 142
Midnight on Beechen 144
The Aërolite 145
The Prospect 147
Genitrix Laesa 148
The Fading Rose 150
When Oats were reaped 152
Louie 153
"She opened the Door" 154
"What's there to tell?" 155
The Harbour Bridge 157
Vagrant's Song 159
Farmer Dunman's Funeral 161
The Sexton at Longpuddle 163
The Harvest-Supper 164
At a Pause in a Country Dance 167

PAGE

On the Portrait of a Woman about to be Hanged 169
The Church and the Wedding 171
The Shiver 173
"Not only I" 175
She saw him, she said 177
Once at Swanage 178
The Flower's Tragedy 179
At the Aquatic Sports 180
A Watcher's Regret 181
Horses aboard 182
The History of an Hour 183
The Missed Train 184
Under High-stoy Hill 186
At the Mill 187
Alike and Unlike 189
The Thing unplanned 190
The Sheep-boy 191
Retty's Phases 193
A Poor Man and a Lady 195
An Expostulation 198
To a Sea-cliff 199
The Echo-elf answers 201
Cynic's Epitaph 202
A Beauty's Soliloquy during her Honeymoon 203
Donaghadee 205
He inadvertently cures his Love-pains 207
The Peace Peal 208
Lady Vi 210
A Popular Personage at Home 212
Inscriptions for a Peal of Eight Bells 214

PAGE

A Refusal 216
Epitaph on a Pessimist 219
The Protean Maiden 220
A Watering-place Lady inventoried 221
The Sea Fight 223
Paradox 224
The Rover come Home 225
"Known had I" 227
The Pat of Butter 228
Bags of Meat 229
The Sundial on a Wet Day 232
Her Haunting-ground 233
A Parting Scene 234
Shortening Days at the Homestead 235
Days to recollect 237
To C. F. H. 239
The High-school Lawn 240
The Forbidden Banns 241
The Paphian Ball 243
On Martock Moor 248
That Moment 250
Premonitions 251
This Summer and Last 252
"Nothing matters much" 254
In the Evening 256
The Six Boards 258
Before my Friend arrived 260
Compassion: an Ode 261
"Why she moved house" 263
Tragedian to Tragedienne 264
The Lady of Forebodings 266

PAGE

THE BIRD-CATCHER'S BOY 267
A HURRIED MEETING 271
DISCOURAGEMENT 275
A LEAVING 276
SONG TO AN OLD BURDEN 277
"WHY DO I?" 279

HUMAN SHOWS
FAR PHANTASIES

WAITING BOTH

A STAR looks down at me,
And says: "Here I and you
Stand, each in our degree:
What do you mean to do,—
Mean to do?"

I say: "For all I know,
Wait, and let Time go by,
Till my change come,"—"Just so,"
The star says: "So mean I:—
So mean I."

A BIRD-SCENE, AT A RURAL DWELLING

WHEN the inmate stirs, the birds retire discreetly
From the window-ledge, whereon they whistled sweetly
And on the step of the door,
In the misty morning hoar;
But now the dweller is up they flee
To the crooked neighbouring codlin-tree;
And when he comes fully forth they seek the garden,
And call from the lofty costard, as pleading pardon
For shouting so near before
In their joy at being alive:—
Meanwhile the hammering clock within goes five.

I know a domicile of brown and green,
Where for a hundred summers there have been
Just such enactments, just such daybreaks seen.

"ANY LITTLE OLD SONG"

ANY little old song
  Will do for me,
Tell it of joys gone long,
  Or joys to be,
Or friendly faces best
  Loved to see.

Newest themes I want not
  On subtle strings,
And for thrillings pant not
  That new song brings:
I only need the homeliest
  Of heartstirrings.

IN A FORMER RESORT AFTER MANY YEARS

DO I know these, slack-shaped and wan,
Whose substance, one time fresh and furrowless,
Is now a rag drawn over a skeleton,
As in El Greco's canvases?—
Whose cheeks have slipped down, lips become indrawn,
And statures shrunk to dwarfishness?

Do they know me, whose former mind
Was like an open plain where no foot falls,
But now is as a gallery portrait-lined,
And scored with necrologic scrawls,
Where feeble voices rise, once full-defined,
From underground in curious calls?

A CATHEDRAL FAÇADE AT MIDNIGHT

ALONG the sculptures of the western wall
I watched the moonlight creeping:
It moved as if it hardly moved at all,
Inch by inch thinly peeping
Round on the pious figures of freestone, brought
And poised there when the Universe was wrought
To serve its centre, Earth, in mankind's thought.

The lunar look skimmed scantly toe, breast, arm,
Then edged on slowly, slightly,
To shoulder, hand, face; till each austere form
Was blanched its whole length brightly
Of prophet, king, queen, cardinal in state,
That dead men's tools had striven to simulate;
And the stiff images stood irradiate.

A frail moan from the martyred saints there set
Mid others of the erection
Against the breeze, seemed sighings of regret
At the ancient faith's rejection
Under the sure, unhasting, steady stress
Of Reason's movement, making meaningless
The coded creeds of old-time godliness.

THE TURNIP-HOER

OF tides that toss the souls of men
Some are foreseen, and weathered warefully;
More burst at flood, none witting why or when,
And are called Destiny.

—Years past there was a turnip-hoer,
Who loved his wife and child, and worked amain
In the turnip-time from dawn till day outwore
And night bedimmed the plain.

The thronging plants of blueish green
Would fall in lanes before his skilful blade,
Which, as by sleight, would deftly slip between
Those spared and those low-laid.

'Twas afternoon: he hoed his best
Unlifting head or eye, when, through the fence,
He heard a gallop dropping from the crest
Of the hill above him, whence,

Descending at a crashing pace,
An open carriage came, horsed by a pair:
A lady sat therein, with lilywhite face
And wildly windblown hair.

The man sprang over, and horse and horse
Faced in the highway as the pair ondrew;
Like Terminus stood he there, and barred their course,
And almost ere he knew

The lady was limp within his arms
And, half-unconscious, clutched his hair and beard;
And so he held her, till from neighbouring farms
Came hinds, and soon appeared

Footman and coachman on the way:—
The steeds were guided back, now breathbespent,
And the hoer was rewarded with good pay:—
So passed the accident.

"She was the Duchess of Southernshire,
They tell me," said the second hoe, next day:
"She's come a-visiting not far from here;
This week will end her stay."

The hoer's wife that evening set
Her hand to a crusted stew in the three-legged pot,
And he sat looking on in silence; yet
The cooking saw he not,

But a woman, with her arms around him,
Glove-handed, clasping his neck and clutching his blouse,
And ere he went to bed that night he found him
Outside a manor-house.

A page there smoking answered him:
"Her Grace's room is where you see that light;
By now she's up there slipping off her trim:
The Dook's is on the right."

She was, indeed, just saying through the door,
"That dauntless fellow saved me from collapse:
I'd not much with me, or 'd have given him more:
'Twas not enough, perhaps!"

Up till she left, before he slept,
He walked, though tired, to where her window shined,
And mused till it went dark; but close he kept
All that was in his mind.

"What is it, Ike?" inquired his wife;
"You are not so nice now as you used to be.
What have I done? You seem quite tired of life!"
"Nothing at all," said he.

In the next shire this lady of rank,
So 'twas made known, would open a bazaar:
He took his money from the savings-bank
To go there, for 'twas far.

And reached her stall, and sighted, clad
In her ripe beauty and the goodliest guise,
His Vision of late. He straight spent all he had,
But not once caught her eyes.

Next week he heard, with heart of clay,
That London held her for three months or so:
Fearing to tell his wife he went for a day,
Pawning his watch to go;

And scanned the Square of her abode,
And timed her moves, as well as he could guess,
That he might glimpse her; till afoot by road
He came home penniless. . . .

—The Duke in Wessex once again,
Glanced at the Wessex paper, where he read
Of a man, late taken to drink, killed by a train
At a crossing, so it said.

"Why—he who saved your life, I
think?"
—"O no," said she. "It cannot be the
same:
He was sweet-breath'd, without a taint of
drink;
Yet it is like his name."

THE CARRIER

"THERE'S a seat, I see, still empty?"
Cried the hailer from the road;
"No there is not!" said the carrier,
Quickening his horse and load.

"—They say you are in the grave, Jane;
But still you ride with me!"
And he looked towards the vacant space
He had kept beside his knee.

And the passengers murmured: " 'Tis where his wife
In journeys to and fro
Used always to sit; but nobody does
Since those long years ago."

Rumble-mumble went the van
Past Sidwell Church and wall,
Till Exon Towers were out of scan,
And night lay over all.

LOVER TO MISTRESS

(SONG)

BECKON to me to come
With handkerchief or hand,
Or finger mere or thumb;
Let forecasts be but rough,
Parents more bleak than bland,
'Twill be enough,
Maid mine,
'Twill be enough!

Two fields, a wood, a tree,
Nothing now more malign
Lies between you and me;
But were they bysm, or bluff,
Or snarling sea, one sign
Would be enough,
Maid mine,
Would be enough!

From an old copy.

THE MONUMENT-MAKER

I CHISELLED her monument
To my mind's content,
Took it to the church by night,
When her planet was at its height,
And set it where I had figured the place in the daytime.
Having niched it there
I stepped back, cheered, and thought its outlines fair,
And its marbles rare.

Then laughed she over my shoulder as in our Maytime:
"It spells not me!" she said:
"Tells nothing about my beauty, wit, or gay time
With all those, quick and dead,
Of high or lowlihead,
That hovered near,
Including you, who carve there your devotion;
But you felt none, my dear!"

And then she vanished. Checkless sprang
my emotion,
And forced a tear
At seeing I'd not been truly known by her,
And never prized!—that my memorial
here,
To consecrate her sepulchre,
Was scorned, almost,
By her sweet ghost:
Yet I hoped not quite, in her very inner-
most!

1916.

CIRCUS-RIDER TO RINGMASTER

WHEN I am riding round the ring no longer,
Tell a tale of me;
Say, no steed-borne woman's nerve was stronger
Than used mine to be.
Let your whole soul say it; do:
O it will be true!

Should I soon no more be mistress found in
Feats I've made my own,
Trace the tan-laid track you'd whip me round in
On the cantering roan:
There may cross your eyes again
My lithe look as then.

Show how I, when clay became my cover,
Took the high-hoop leap
Into your arms, who coaxed and grew my lover,—
Ah, to make me weep
Since those claspings cared for so
Ever so long ago!

Though not now as when you freshly
knew me,
But a fading form,
Shape the kiss you'd briskly blow up to me
While our love was warm,
And my cheek unstained by tears,
As in these last years!

LAST WEEK IN OCTOBER

THE trees are undressing, and fling in many places—
On the gray road, the roof, the window-sill—
Their radiant robes and ribbons and yellow laces;
A leaf each second so is flung at will,
Here, there, another and another, still and still.

A spider's web has caught one while downcoming,
That stays there dangling when the rest pass on;
Like a suspended criminal hangs he, mumming
In golden garb, while one yet green, high yon,
Trembles, as fearing such a fate for himself anon.

COME NOT; YET COME!

(SONG)

IN my sage moments I can say,
Come not near,
But far in foreign regions stay,
So that here
A mind may grow again serene and clear.

But the thought withers. Why should I
Have fear to earn me
Fame from your nearness, though thereby
Old fires new burn me,
And lastly, maybe, tear and overturn me!

So I say, Come: deign again shine
Upon this place,
Even if unslackened smart be mine
From that sweet face,
And I faint to a phantom past all trace.

THE LATER AUTUMN

GONE are the lovers, under the bush
Stretched at their ease;
Gone the bees,
Tangling themselves in your hair as they rush
On the line of your track,
Leg-laden, back
With a dip to their hive
In a prepossessed dive.

Toadsmeat is mangy, frosted, and sere;
Apples in grass
Crunch as we pass,
And rot ere the men who make cyder appear.
Couch-fires abound
On fallows around,
And shades far extend
Like lives soon to end.

Spinning leaves join the remains shrunk
and brown
Of last year's display
That lie wasting away,
On whose corpses they earlier as scorners
gazed down
From their aery green height:
Now in the same plight
They huddle; while yon
A robin looks on.

"LET ME"

(SONG)

LET me believe it, dearest,
Let it be
As just a dream—the merest—
Haunting me,
That a frank full-souled sweetness
Warmed your smile
And voice, to indiscreetness
Once, awhile!

And I will fondly ponder
Till I lie
Earthed up with others yonder
Past a sigh,
That you may name at stray times
With regret
One whom through green and gray times
You forget!

AT A FASHIONABLE DINNER

WE sat with the banqueting-party
By the table-end—
Unmarked,—no diners out
Were we: scarce a friend
Of our own mind's trend
Was there, though the welcome was hearty.
Then we noticed a shade extend
By a distant screen,
And I said: "What to you does it seem to mean,
Lavine?"

"—It is like my own body lying
Beyond the door
Where the servants glide in and about
The carpeted floor;
And it means my death hour!—"
"—What a fancy! Who feels like dying
While these smart sallies pour,
With laughter between!
To me it is more like satin sheen,
Lavine."

"—That means your new bride, when
you win her:
Yes, so it must be!
It's her satin dress, no doubt—
That shine you see—
My own corpse to me!"
And a gloom came over the dinner,
Where almost strangers were we,
As the spirit of the scene
Forsook her—the fairest of the whole
thirteen—
Lavine!

GREEN SLATES

(PENPETHY)

IT happened once, before the duller
Loomings of life defined them,
I searched for slates of greenish colour
A quarry where men mined them;

And saw, the while I peered around there,
In the quarry standing
A form against the slate background there,
Of fairness eye-commanding.

And now, though fifty years have flown me,
With all their dreams and duties,
And strange-pipped dice my hand has thrown me,
And dust are all her beauties,

Green slates—seen high on roofs, or lower
In waggon, truck, or lorry—
Cry out: "Our home was where you saw her
Standing in the quarry!"

AN EAST-END CURATE

A SMALL blind street off East
Commercial Road;
Window, door; window, door;
Every house like the one before,
Is where the curate, Mr. Dowle, has found
a pinched abode.
Spectacled, pale, moustache straw-coloured,
and with a long thin face,
Day or dark his lodgings' narrow doorstep
does he pace.

A bleached pianoforte, with its drawn silk
plaitings faded,
Stands in his room, its keys much yellowed,
cyphering, and abraded,
"Novello's Anthems" lie at hand, and also
a few glees,
And "Laws of Heaven for Earth" in a
frame upon the wall one sees.

He goes through his neighbours' houses as
his own, and none regards,
And opens their back-doors off-hand, to
look for them in their yards:
A man is threatening his wife on the other
side of the wall,
But the curate lets it pass as knowing the
history of it all.

Freely within his hearing the children skip
and laugh and say:
"There's Mister Dow-well! There's
Mister Dow-well!" in their play;
And the long, pallid, devoted face
notes not,
But stoops along abstractedly, for good, or
in vain, God wot!

AT RUSHY-POND

ON the frigid face of the heath-hemmed pond
There shaped the half-grown moon:
Winged whiffs from the north with a husky croon
Blew over and beyond.

And the wind flapped the moon in its float on the pool,
And stretched it to oval form;
Then corkscrewed it like a wriggling worm;
Then wanned it weariful.

And I cared not for conning the sky above
Where hung the substant thing,
For my thought was earthward sojourning
On the scene I had vision of.

Since there it was once, in a secret year,
I had called a woman to me
From across this water, ardently—
And practised to keep her near;

Till the last weak love-words had been said,
And ended was her time,
And blurred the bloomage of her prime,
And white the earlier red.

And the troubled orb in the pond's sad shine
Was her very wraith, as scanned
When she withdrew thence, mirrored, and
Her days dropped out of mine.

FOUR IN THE MORNING

AT four this day of June I rise:
The dawn-light strengthens steadily;
Earth is a cerule mystery,
As if not far from Paradise
At four o'clock,

Or else in the Great Nebula,
Or where the Pleiads blink and smile:
(For though we see with eyes of guile
The grisly grin of things by day,
At four o'clock

They show their best.) . . . In this vale's space
I am up the first, I think. Yet, no,
A whistling? and the to-and-fro
Wheezed whettings of a scythe apace
At four o'clock? . . .

—Though pleasure spurred, I rose with
irk:
Here is one at compulsion's whip
Taking his life's stern stewardship
With blithe uncare, and hard at work
At four o'clock!

Bockhampton.

ON THE ESPLANADE

MIDSUMMER: 10 P.M.

THE broad bald moon edged up where
the sea was wide,
Mild, mellow-faced;
Beneath, a tumbling twinkle of shines,
like dyed,
A trackway traced
To the shore, as of petals fallen from a
rose to waste,
In its overblow,
And fluttering afloat on inward heaves of
the tide :—
All this, so plain ; yet the rest I did not
know.

The horizon gets lost in a mist new-wrought
by the night :
The lamps of the Bay
That reach from behind me round to the
left and right
On the sea-wall way

For a constant mile of curve, make a long display
As a pearl-strung row,
Under which in the waves they bore their gimlets of light:—
All this was plain; but there was a thing not so.

Inside a window, open, with undrawn blind,
There plays and sings
A lady unseen a melody undefined:
And where the moon flings
Its shimmer a vessel crosses, whereon to the strings
Plucked sweetly and low
Of a harp, they dance. Yea, such did I mark. That, behind,
My Fate's masked face crept near me I did not know!

IN ST. PAUL'S A WHILE AGO

SUMMER and winter close commune
On this July afternoon
As I enter chilly Paul's,
With its chasmal classic walls.
—Drifts of gray illumination
From the lofty fenestration
Slant them down in bristling spines that spread
Fan-like upon the vast dust-moted shade.

Moveless here, no whit allied
To the daemonian din outside,
Statues stand, cadaverous, wan,
Round the loiterers looking on
Under the yawning dome and nave,
Pondering whatnot, giddy or grave.
Here a verger moves a chair,
Or a red rope fixes there:—
A brimming Hebe, rapt in her adorning,
Brushes an Artemisia craped in mourning;

Beatrice Benedick piques, coquetting;
All unknowing or forgetting
That strange Jew, Damascus-bound,
Whose name, thereafter travelling round
To this precinct of the world,
Spread here like a flag unfurled:
Anon inspiring architectural sages
To frame this pile, writ his throughout the ages:
Whence also the encircling mart
Assumed his name, of him no part,
And to his vision-seeing mind
Charmless, blank in every kind;
And whose displays, even had they called his eye,
No gold or silver had been his to buy;
Whose haunters, had they seen him stand
On his own steps here, lift his hand
In stress of eager, stammering speech,
And his meaning chanced to reach,
Would have proclaimed him as they passed
An epilept enthusiast.

COMING UP OXFORD STREET: EVENING

THE sun from the west glares back,
And the sun from the watered track,
And the sun from the sheets of glass,
And the sun from each window-brass;
Sun-mirrorings, too, brighten
From show-cases beneath
The laughing eyes and teeth
Of ladies who rouge and whiten.
And the same warm god explores
Panels and chinks of doors;
Problems with chymists' bottles
Profound as Aristotle's
He solves, and with good cause,
Having been ere man was.

Also he dazzles the pupils of one who walks west,
A city-clerk, with eyesight not of the best,

38 OXFORD STREET: EVENING

Who sees no escape to the very verge of
his days
From the rut of Oxford Street into open
ways;
And he goes along with head and eyes
flagging forlorn,
Empty of interest in things, and wondering
why he was born.

As seen July 4, 1872.

A LAST JOURNEY

"FATHER, you seem to have
been sleeping fair?"
The child uncovered the dimity-curtained
window-square
And looked out at the dawn,
And back at the dying man nigh gone,
And propped up in his chair,
Whose breathing a robin's "chink" took
up in antiphon.

The open fireplace spread
Like a vast weary yawn above his head,
Its thin blue blower waved against his
whitening crown,
For he could not lie down:
He raised him on his arms so emaci-
ated:—

"Yes; I've slept long, my child. But as for rest,
Well, that I cannot say.
The whole night have I footed field and turnpike-way—
A regular pilgrimage—as at my best
And very briskest day!

"'Twas first to Weatherb'ry, to see them there,
And thence to King's-Stag, where
I joined in a jolly trip to Weydon-Priors Fair:
I shot for nuts, bought gingerbreads, cream-cheese;
And, not content with these,
I went to London: heard the watchmen cry the hours.

"I soon was off again, and found me in the bowers
Of father's apple-trees,
And he shook the apples down: they fell in showers,
Whereon he turned, smiled strange at me, as ill at ease;
And then you pulled the curtain; and, ah me,
I found me back where I wished not to be!"

'Twas told the child next day: "Your
father's dead."
And, struck, she questioned, "O,
That journey, then, did father really
go ?—
Buy nuts, and cakes, and travel at night
till dawn was red,
And tire himself with journeying, as he
said,
To see those old friends that he cared
for so?"

SINGING LOVERS

I ROWED: the dimpled tide was at the turn,
And mirth and moonlight spread upon the bay:
There were two singing lovers in the stern;
But mine had gone away,—
Whither, I shunned to say !

The houses stood confronting us afar,
A livid line against the evening glare;
The small lamps livened; then out-stole a star;
But my Love was not there,—
Vanished, I sorrowed where!

His arm was round her, both full facing me
With no reserve. Theirs was not love to hide;
He held one tiller-rope, the other she;
I pulled—the merest glide,—
Looked on at them, and sighed.

The moon's glassed glory heaved as we
lay swinging
Upon the undulations. Shoreward, slow,
The plash of pebbles joined the lovers'
singing,
But she of a bygone vow
Joined in the song not now!

Weymouth.

THE MONTH'S CALENDAR

TEAR off the calendar
Of this month past,
And all its weeks, that are
Flown, to be cast
To oblivion fast!

Darken that day
On which we met,
With its words of gay
Half-felt regret
That you'll forget!

The second day, too;
The noon I nursed
Well—thoughts; yes, through
To the thirty-first;
That was the worst.

For then it was
You let me see
There was good cause
Why you could not be
Aught ever to me!

A SPELLBOUND PALACE

(HAMPTON COURT)

ON this kindly yellow day of mild low-
travelling winter sun
The stirless depths of the yews
Are vague with misty blues:
Across the spacious pathways stretching
spires of shadow run,
And the wind-gnawed walls of ancient
brick are fired vermilion.

Two or three early sanguine finches
tune
Some tentative strains, to be enlarged
by May or June:
From a thrush or blackbird
Comes now and then a word,
While an enfeebled fountain somewhere
within is heard.

Our footsteps wait awhile,
Then draw beneath the pile,
When an inner court outspreads
As 'twere History's own aisle,

Where the now-visioned fountain its attenuate crystal sheds
In passive lapse that seems to ignore the yon world's clamorous clutch,
And lays an insistent stillness on the place, like a cold hand's touch.

And there swaggers the Shade of a straddling King, plumed, sworded, with sensual face,
And lo, too, that of his Minister, at a bold self-centred pace:
Sheer in the sun they pass; and thereupon all is still,
Save the mindless fountain tinkling on with thin enfeebled will.

WHEN DEAD

TO ———

IT will be much better when
I am under the bough;
I shall be more myself, Dear, then,
Than I am now.

No sign of querulousness
To wear you out
Shall I show there: strivings and stress
Be quite without.

This fleeting life-brief blight
Will have gone past
When I resume my old and right
Place in the Vast.

And when you come to me
To show you true,
Doubt not I shall infallibly
Be waiting you.

SINE PROLE

(MEDIAEVAL LATIN SEQUENCE-METRE)

FORTH from ages thick in mystery,
Through the morn and noon of history,
To the moment where I stand
Has my line wound; I the last one—
Outcome of each spectral past one
Of that file, so many-manned!

Nothing in its time-trail marred it:
As one long life I regard it
Throughout all the years till now,
When it fain—the close seen coming—
After annals past all plumbing—
Makes to Being its parting bow.

Unlike Jahveh's ancient nation,
Little in their line's cessation
Moderns see for surge of sighs:
They have been schooled by lengthier vision,
View Life's lottery with misprision,
And its dice that fling no prize!

TEN YEARS SINCE

'TIS ten years since
I saw her on the stairs,
Heard her in house-affairs,
And listened to her cares;
And the trees are ten feet taller,
And the sunny spaces smaller
Whose bloomage would enthrall her;
And the piano wires are rustier,
The smell of bindings mustier,
And lofts and lumber dustier
Than when, with casual look
And ear, light note I took
Of what shut like a book
Those ten years since!

Nov., 1922.

EVERY ARTEMISIA

"YOUR eye-light wanes with an ail of
care,
Frets freeze gray your face and hair."

"I was the woman who met him,
Then cool and keen,
Whiling away
Time, with its restless scene on scene
Every day."

"Your features fashion as in a dream
Of things that were, or used to seem."

"I was the woman who won him:
Steadfast and fond
Was he, while I
Tepidly took what he gave, nor conned
Wherefore or why."

"Your house looks blistered by a curse,
As if a wraith ruled there, or worse."

"I was the woman who slighted him:
Far from my town
Into the night
He went. . . . My hair, then auburn-brown,
Pangs have wanned white."

"Your ways reflect a monstrous gloom;
Your voice speaks from within a tomb."

"I was the woman who buried him:
My misery
God laughed to scorn:
The people said: ''Twere well if she
Had not been born!' "

"You plod to pile a monument
So madly that your breath is spent."

"I am the woman who god him:
I build, to ease
My scalding fires,
A temple topping the Deities'
Fanes of my sires."

THE BEST SHE COULD

NINE leaves a minute
Swim down shakily;
Each one fain would spin it
Straight to earth; but, see,
How the sharp airs win it
Slantwise away!—Hear it say,
"Now we have finished our summer show
Of what we knew the way to do:
Alas, not much! But, as things go,
As fair as any. And night-time calls,
And the curtain falls!"

Sunlight goes on shining
As if no frost were here,
Blackbirds seem designing
Where to build next year;
Yet is warmth declining:
And still the day seems to say,

"Saw you how Dame Summer drest?
Of all God taught her she bethought her!
Alas, not much! And yet the best
She could, within the too short time
Granted her prime."

Nov. 8, 1923.

THE GRAVEYARD OF DEAD CREEDS

I LIT upon the graveyard of dead creeds
In wistful wanderings through old wastes of thought,
Where bristled fennish fungi, fruiting nought,
Amid the sepulchres begirt with weeds,

Which stone by stone recorded sanct, deceased
Catholicons that had, in centuries flown,
Physicked created man through his long groan,
Ere they went under, all their potence ceased.

When in a breath-while, lo, their spectres rose
Like wakened winds that autumn summons up:—

"Out of us cometh an heir, that shall disclose
New promise!" cried they. "And the caustic cup

"We ignorantly upheld to men, be filled
With draughts more pure than those we ever distilled,
That shall make tolerable to sentient seers
The melancholy marching of the years."

"THERE SEEMED A STRANGENESS"

A PHANTASY

THERE seemed a strangeness in the air,
Vermilion light on the land's lean face;
I heard a Voice from I knew not where:—
"The Great Adjustment is taking place!

"I set thick darkness over you,
And fogged you all your years therein;
At last I uncloud your view,
Which I am weary of holding in.

"Men have not heard, men have not seen
Since the beginning of the world
What earth and heaven mean;
But now their curtains shall be furled,

"And they shall see what is, ere long,
Not through a glass, but face to face;
And Right shall disestablish Wrong:
The Great Adjustment is taking place."

A NIGHT OF QUESTIONINGS

ON the eve of All-Souls' Day
I heard the dead men say
Who lie by the tottering tower,
To the dark and doubling wind
At the midnight's turning hour,
When other speech had thinned:
"What of the world now?"
The wind whiffed back: "Men still
Who are born, do good, do ill
Here, just as in your time:
Till their years the locust hath eaten,
Leaving them bare, downbeaten;
Somewhiles in springtide rime,
Somewhiles in summer glow,
Somewhiles in winter snow:—
No more I know."

The same eve I caught cry
To the selfsame wind, those dry

As dust beneath the aisles
Of old cathedral piles,
Walled up in vaulted biers
Through many Christian years:
  "What of the world now?"
Sighed back the circuiteer:
"Men since your time, shrined here
By deserved ordinance,
Their own craft, or by chance,
Which follows men from birth
Even until under earth,
But little difference show
When ranged in sculptured row,
Different as dyes although:—
    No more I know."

On the selfsame eve, too, said
Those swayed in the sunk sea-bed
To the selfsame wind as it played
With the tide in the starless shade
From Comorin to Horn,
And round by Wrath forlorn:
  "What of the world now?"
And the wind for a second ceased,
Then whirred: "Men west and east,
As each sun soars and dips,
Go down to the sea in ships
As you went—hither and thither;
See the wonders of the deep,
As you did, ere they sleep;

But few at home care whither
They wander to and fro;
Themselves care little also!—
    No more I know."

Said, too, on the selfsame eve
The troubled skulls that heave
And fust in the flats of France,
To the wind wayfaring over
Listlessly as in trance
From the Ardennes to Dover,
  "What of the world now?"
And the farer moaned: "As when
You mauled these fields, do men
Set them with dark-drawn breaths
To knave their neighbours' deaths
In periodic spasms!
Yea, fooled by foul phantasms,
In a strange cyclic throe
Backward to type they go:—
    No more I know."

That night, too, men whose crimes
Had cut them off betimes,
Who lay within the pales
Of town and county jails
With the rope-groove on them yet,
Said to the same wind's fret
  "What of the world now?"

And the blast in its brooding tone
Returned: "Men have not shown,
Since you were stretched that morning,
A white cap your adorning,
More lovely deeds or true
Through thus neck-knotting you;
Or that they purer grow,
Or ever will, I trow!—
No more I know."

XENOPHANES, THE MONIST OF COLOPHON

ANN: AET: SUAE XCII.—A: C: CCCCLXXX.

"ARE You groping Your way?
Do You do it unknowing?—
Or mark Your wind blowing?
Night tell You from day,
O Mover? Come, say!"
Cried Xenophanes.

"I mean, querying so,
Do You do it aware,
Or by rote, like a player,
Or in ignorance, nor care
Whether doing or no?"
Pressed Xenophanes.

"Thus strive I to plumb
Your depths, O Great Dumb!—
Not a god, but the All

(As I read) ; yet a thrall
To a blind ritual,"
Sighed Xenophanes.

"If I only could bring
You to own it, close Thing,
I would write it again
With a still stronger pen
To my once neighbour-men!"
Said Xenophanes.

—Quoth the listening Years:
"You ask It in vain;
You waste sighs and tears
On these callings inane,
Which It grasps not nor hears,
O Xenophanes!"

"When you penned what you thought
You were cast out, and sought
A retreat over sea
From aroused enmity:
So it always will be,
Yea, Xenophanes!

"In the lone of the nights
At Elea unseen,
Where the swinging wave smites
Of the restless Tyrrhene,
You may muse thus, serene,
Safe, Xenophanes.

"But write it not back
To your dear Colophon;
Brows still will be black
At your words, 'All is One,'
From disputers thereon,
Know, Xenophanes.

"Three thousand years hence,
Men who hazard a clue
To this riddle immense,
And still treat it as new,
Will be scowled at, like you,
O Xenophanes!

" '*Some day I may tell,*
When I've broken My spell,'
It snores in Its sleep
If you listen long, deep
At Its closely-sealed cell,
Wronged Xenophanes!

"Yea, on, near the end,
Its doings may mend;
Aye, when you're forgotten,
And old cults are rotten,
And bulky codes shotten,
Xenophanes!"

1921.

LIFE AND DEATH AT SUNRISE

(NEAR DOGBURY GATE, 1867)

THE hills uncap their tops
Of woodland, pasture, copse,
And look on the layers of mist
At their foot that still persist:
They are like awakened sleepers on one elbow lifted,
Who gaze around to learn if things during night have shifted.

A waggon creaks up from the fog
With a laboured leisurely jog;
Then a horseman from off the hill-tip
Comes clapping down into the dip;
While woodlarks, finches, sparrows, try to entune at one time,
And cocks and hens and cows and bulls take up the chime.

With a shouldered basket and flagon
A man meets the one with the waggon,

And both the men halt of long use.
"Well," the waggoner says, "what's the news?"
"—'Tis a boy this time. You've just met the doctor trotting back.
She's doing very well. And we think we shall call him 'Jack.'

"And what have you got covered there?"
He nods to the waggon and mare.
"Oh, a coffin for old John Thinn:
We are just going to put him in."
"—So he's gone at last. He always had a good constitution."
"—He was ninety-odd. He could call up the French Revolution."

NIGHT-TIME IN MID-FALL

IT is a storm-strid night, winds footing swift
Through the blind profound;
I know the happenings from their sound;
Leaves totter down still green, and spin and drift;
The tree-trunks rock to their roots, which wrench and lift
The loam where they run onward underground.

The streams are muddy and swollen; eels migrate
To a new abode;
Even cross, 'tis said, the turnpike-road;
(Men's feet have felt their crawl, homecoming late):
The westward fronts of towers are saturate,
Church-timbers crack, and witches ride abroad.

A SHEEP FAIR

THE day arrives of the autumn fair,
And torrents fall,
Though sheep in throngs are gathered there,
Ten thousand all,
Sodden, with hurdles round them reared:
And, lot by lot, the pens are cleared,
And the auctioneer wrings out his beard,
And wipes his book, bedrenched and smeared,
And rakes the rain from his face with the edge of his hand,
As torrents fall.

The wool of the ewes is like a sponge
With the daylong rain:
Jammed tight, to turn, or lie, or lunge,
They strive in vain.

Their horns are soft as finger-nails,
Their shepherds reek against the rails,
The tied dogs soak with tucked-in tails,
The buyers' hat-brims fill like pails,
Which spill small cascades when they shift their stand
In the daylong rain.

POSTSCRIPT

Time has trailed lengthily since met
At Pummery Fair
Those panting thousands in their wet
And woolly wear:
And every flock long since has bled,
And all the dripping buyers have sped,
And the hoarse auctioneer is dead,
Who "Going—going!" so often said,
As he consigned to doom each meek, mewed band
At Pummery Fair.

SNOW IN THE SUBURBS

EVERY branch big with it,
Bent every twig with it;
Every fork like a white web-foot;
Every street and pavement mute:
Some flakes have lost their way, and grope back upward, when
Meeting those meandering down they turn and descend again.
The palings are glued together like a wall,
And there is no waft of wind with the fleecy fall.

A sparrow enters the tree,
Whereon immediately
A snow-lump thrice his own slight size
Descends on him and showers his head and eyes,

And overturns him,
And near inurns him,
And lights on a nether twig, when its brush
Starts off a volley of other lodging lumps with a rush.

The steps are a blanched slope,
Up which, with feeble hope,
A black cat comes, wide-eyed and thin;
And we take him in.

A LIGHT SNOW-FALL AFTER FROST

ON the flat road a man at last appears:
How much his whitening hairs
Owe to the settling snow's mute anchorage,
And how much to a life's rough pilgrimage,
One cannot certify.

The frost is on the wane,
And cobwebs hanging close outside the pane
Pose as festoons of thick white worsted there,
Of their pale presence no eye being aware
Till the rime made them plain.

A second man comes by;
His ruddy beard brings fire to the pallid scene:
His coat is faded green;
Hence seems it that his mien
Wears something of the dye
Of the berried holm-trees that he passes nigh.

The snow-feathers so gently swoop that though
But half an hour ago
The road was brown, and now is starkly white,
A watcher would have failed defining quite
When it transformed it so.

Near Surbiton.

WINTER NIGHT IN WOODLAND

(OLD TIME)

THE bark of a fox rings, sonorous
and long:—
Three barks, and then silentness;
"wong, wong, wong!"
In quality horn-like, yet melancholy,
As from teachings of years; for an
old one is he.
The hand of all men is against him, he
knows; and yet, why?
That he knows not,—will never know,
down to his death-halloo cry.

With clap-nets and lanterns off start
the bird-baiters,
In trim to make raids on the roosts in
the copse,
Where they beat the boughs artfully,
while their awaiters
Grow heavy at home over divers
warm drops.

The poachers, with swingels, and matches
of brimstone, outcreep
To steal upon pheasants and drowse them
a-perch and asleep.

Out there, on the verge, where a path
wavers through,
Dark figures, filed singly, thrid quickly
the view,
Yet heavily laden: land-carriers are
they
In the hire of the smugglers from
some nearest bay.
Each bears his two "tubs," slung across,
one in front, one behind,
To a further snug hiding, which none but
themselves are to find.

And then, when the night has turned
twelve the air brings
From dim distance, a rhythm of
voices and strings:
'Tis the quire, just afoot on their long
yearly rounds,
To rouse by worn carols each house
in their bounds;
Robert Penny, the Dewys, Mail, Voss,
and the rest; till anon
Tired and thirsty, but cheerful, they home
to their beds in the dawn.

ICE ON THE HIGHWAY

SEVEN buxom women abreast, and arm in arm,
Trudge down the hill, tip-toed,
And breathing warm;
They must perforce trudge thus, to keep upright
On the glassy ice-bound road,
And they must get to market whether or no,
Provisions running low
With the nearing Saturday night,
While the lumbering van wherein they mostly ride
Can nowise go:
Yet loud their laughter as they stagger and slide!

Yell'ham Hill.

MUSIC IN A SNOWY STREET

THE weather is sharp,
But the girls are unmoved:
One wakes from a harp,
The next from a viol
A strain that I loved
When life was no trial.

The tripletime beat
Bounds forth on the snow,
But the spry springing feet
Of a century ago,
And the arms that enlaced
As the couples embraced,
Are silent old bones
Under graying gravestones.

The snow-feathers sail
Across the harp-strings,
Whose throbbing threads wail
Like love-satiate things.

Each lyre's grimy mien,
With its rout-raising tune,
Against the new white
Of the flake-laden noon,
Is incongruous to sight,
Hinting years they have seen
Of revel at night
Ere these damsels became
Possessed of their frame.

O bygone whirls, heys,
Crotchets, quavers, the same
That were danced in the days
Of grim Bonaparte's fame,
Or even by the toes
Of the fair Antoinette,—
Yea, old notes like those
Here are living on yet!—
But of their fame and fashion
How little these know
Who strum without passion
For pence, in the snow!

THE FROZEN GREENHOUSE

(ST. JULIOT)

"THERE was a frost
Last night!" she said,
"And the stove was forgot
When we went to bed,
And the greenhouse plants
Are frozen dead!"

By the breakfast blaze
Blank-faced spoke she,
Her scared young look
Seeming to be
The very symbol
Of tragedy.

The frost is fiercer
Than then to-day,
As I pass the place
Of her once dismay,
But the greenhouse stands
Warm, tight, and gay,

While she who grieved
At the sad lot
Of her pretty plants—
Cold, iced, forgot—
Herself is colder,
And knows it not.

TWO LIPS

I KISSED them in fancy as I came
Away in the morning glow:
I kissed them through the glass of her picture-frame:
She did not know.

I kissed them in love, in troth, in laughter
When she knew all; long so!
That I should kiss them in a shroud thereafter
She did not know.

NO BUYERS

A STREET SCENE

A LOAD of brushes and baskets
and cradles and chairs
Labours along the street in the
rain:
With it a man, a woman, a pony with
whiteybrown hairs.—
The man foots in front of the horse
with a shambling sway
At a slower tread than a funeral
train,
While to a dirge-like tune he chants
his wares,
Swinging a Turk's-head brush (in a drum-
major's way
When the bandsmen march
and play).

A yard from the back of the man is the
whiteybrown pony's nose:
He mirrors his master in every item of pace
and pose:

He stops when the man stops,
without being told,
And seems to be eased by a pause;
too plainly he's old,
Indeed, not strength enough
shows
To steer the disjointed waggon
straight,
Which wriggles left and right in a
rambling line,
Deflected thus by its own warp and
weight,
And pushing the pony with it in each
incline.

The woman walks on the pave-
ment verge,
Parallel to the man:
She wears an apron white and wide
in span,
And carries a like Turk's-head, but more
in nursing-wise:
Now and then she joins in his
dirge,
But as if her thoughts were on
distant things.
The rain clams her apron till it
clings.—
So, step by step, they move with
their merchandize,
And nobody buys.

ONE WHO MARRIED ABOVE HIM

"'TIS you, I think? Back from
your week's work, Steve?"

"It is I. Back from work this
Christmas Eve."

"But you seem off again?—in this
night-rime?"

"I am off again, and thoroughly off
this time."

"What does that mean?"

"More than may first be seen. . .

Half an hour ago I footed homeward
here,
No wife found I, nor child, nor maid,
indoors or near.

She has, as always, gone with them to her
mother's at the farm,
Where they fare better far than here, and,
maybe, meet less harm.
She's left no fire, no light, has cooked
me nothing to eat,
Though she had fuel, and money to get
some Christmas meat.
Christmas with them is grand, she
knows, and brings good victual,
Other than how it is here, where it's but
lean and little.
But though not much, and rough,
If managed neat there's enough.
She and hers are too highmade for
me;
But she's whimmed her once too often,
she'll see!
Farmer Bollen's daughter should never
have married a man that's poor;
And I can stand it no longer; I'm
leaving; you'll see me no more, be
sure."

"But nonsense: you'll be back again ere
bedtime, and lighting a fire,
And sizzling your supper, and vexing
not that her views of supper are
higher."

"Never for me."

"Well, we shall see."

The sceptical neighbour and Stephen then
followed their foredesigned ways,
And their steps dimmed into white silence
upon the slippery glaze;
And the trees went on with their spitting
amid the icicled haze.

The evening whiled, and the wife with
the babies came home,
But he was not there, nor all Christmas
Day did he come.
Christmastide went, and likewise went
the New Year.
But no husband's footfall revived,
And month after month lapsed, gray-
time to green and to sere,
And other new years arrived,
And the children grew up: one hus-
banded and one wived.—
She wept and repented,
But Stephen never relented.
And there stands the house, and the
sycamore-tree and all,
With its roots forming steps for the
passers who care to call,

And there are the mullioned windows,
and Ham-Hill door,
Through which Steve's wife was brought
out, but which Steve re-entered
no more.

THE NEW TOY

SHE cannot leave it alone,
The new toy;
She pats it, smooths it, rights it, to show it's her own,
As the other train-passengers muse on its temper and tone,
Till she draws from it cries of annoy:—
She feigns to appear as if thinking it nothing so rare
Or worthy of pride, to achieve
This wonder a child, though with reason the rest of them there
May so be inclined to believe.

QUEEN CAROLINE TO HER GUESTS

DEAR friends, stay!
Lamplit wafts of wit keep sorrow
In the purlieus of to-morrow:
Dear friends, stay!

Haste not away!
Even now may Time be weaving
Tricks of ravage, wrack, bereaving,
Haste not away!

Through the pane,
Lurking along the street, there may be
Heartwrings, keeping hid till day be,
Through the pane.

Check their reign:
Since while here we are the masters,
And can barricade dim disasters:
Check their reign!

Give no ear
To those ghosts withoutside mumming,
Mouthing, threatening, "We are coming!"
Give no ear!

Sheltered here
Care we not that next day bring us
Pains, perversions! No racks wring us
Sheltered here.

Homeward gone,
Sleep will slay this merrymaking;
No resuming it at waking,
Homeward gone.

After dawn
Something sad may be befalling;
Mood like ours there's no recalling
After dawn!

Morrow-day
Present joy that moments strengthen
May be past our power to lengthen,
Morrow-day!

Dear friends, stay!
Lamplit wafts of wit keep sorrow
In the limbo of to-morrow;
Dear friends, stay!

PLENA TIMORIS

THE lovers looked over the parapet-stone:
The moon in its southing directly blent
Its silver with their environment.
Her ear-rings twinkled; her teeth, too, shone
As, his arm around her, they laughed and leant.

A man came up to them; then one more.
"There's a woman in the canal below,"
They said; climbed over; slid down; let go,
And a splashing was heard, till an arm upbore,
And a dripping body began to show.

"Drowned herself for love of a man,
Who at one time used to meet her here,
Until he grew tired. But she'd wait him near,
And hope, till hopeless despair began.
So much for love in this mortal sphere!"

The girl's heart shuddered; it seemed as to freeze her
That here, at their tryst for so many a day,
Another woman's tragedy lay.
Dim dreads of the future grew slowly to seize her,
And her arm dropt from his as they wandered away.

THE WEARY WALKER

A PLAIN in front of me,
And there's the road
Upon it. Wide country,
And, too, the road!

Past the first ridge another,
And still the road
Creeps on. Perhaps no other
Ridge for the road?

Ah! Past that ridge a third,
Which still the road
Has to climb furtherward—
The thin white road!

Sky seems to end its track;
But no. The road
Trails down the hill at the back.
Ever the road!

LAST LOVE-WORD

(SONG)

THIS is the last; the very, very last!
Anon, and all is dead and dumb,
Only a pale shroud over the past,
That cannot be
Of value small or vast,
Love, then to me!

I can say no more: I have even said too much.
I did not mean that this should come:
I did not know 'twould swell to such—
Nor, perhaps, you—
When that first look and touch,
Love, doomed us two!

189–.

NOBODY COMES

TREE-LEAVES labour up and down,
And through them the fainting light
Succumbs to the crawl of night.
Outside in the road the telegraph wire
To the town from the darkening land
Intones to travellers like a spectral lyre
Swept by a spectral hand.

A car comes up, with lamps full-glare,
That flash upon a tree:
It has nothing to do with me,
And whangs along in a world of its own,
Leaving a blacker air;
And mute by the gate I stand again alone,
And nobody pulls up there.

October 9, 1924.

IN THE STREET

(SONG)

ONLY acquaintances
Seem do we,
Each of whom, meeting, says
Civilly
"Good morning."—Yes: thus we appear
to be!

But far, near, left and right,
Here or there,
By day or dingiest night,
Everywhere
I see you: one incomparably fair!

So do we wend our ways,
Beautiful girl,
Along our parallel days;
While unfurl
Our futures, and what there may whelm
and whirl.

THE LAST LEAF

"THE leaves throng thick above:—
Well, I'll come back, dear Love,
When they all are down!"

She watched that August tree,
(None now scorned summer as she),
Till it broidered it brown.

And then October came blowing,
And the leaves showed signs they were going,
And she saw up through them.

O how she counted them then!
—November left her but ten,
And started to strew them.

"Ah, when they all are gone,
And the skeleton-time comes on,
Whom shall I see!"

—When the fifteenth spread its sky
That month, her upturned eye
Could count but three.

And at the close of the week
A flush flapped over her cheek:
The last one fell.

But—he did not come. And, at length,
Her hope of him lost all strength,
And it was as a knell. . . .

When he did come again,
Years later, a husband then,
Heavy somewhat,

With a smile she reminded him:
And he cried: "Ah, that vow of our whim!—
Which I forgot,

"As one does!—And was that the tree?
So it was!—Dear me, dear me:
Yes: I forgot."

AT WYNYARD'S GAP

SHE (*on horseback*)

THE hounds pass here?

HE (*on horseback*)

They did an hour ago,
Just in full cry, and went down-wind, I saw,
Towards Pen Wood, where they may kill, and draw
A second time, and bear towards the Yeo.

SHE

How vexing! And I've crept along unthinking.

HE

Ah!—lost in dreams. Fancy to fancy linking!

SHE (*more softly*)

Not that, quite. . . . Now, to settle what I'll do.

HE

Go home again. But have you seen the view
From the top there? Not? It's really worth your while.—
You must dismount, because there is a stile.

They dismount, hitch their horses, and climb a few-score yards from the road.

There you see half South Wessex,—combe, and glen,
And down, to Lewsdon Hill and Pilsdon Pen.

SHE

Yes. It is fine. And I, though living out there
By Crewkerne, never knew it. (*She turns her head*) Well, I declare,
Look at the horses!—How shall I catch my mare?

The horses have got loose and scampered off.

Now that's your fault, through leading me up here!
You must have known 'twould happen—

HE

No, my dear!

SHE

I'm not your dear.

HE (*blandly*)

But you can't help being so,
If it comes to that. The fairest girl I've seen
Is of course dear—by her own fault, I mean.

SHE (*quickly*)

What house is that we see just down below?

HE

Oh—that's the inn called "Wynyard's Gap."—I'll go
While you wait here, and catch those brutes. Don't stir.

He goes. She waits.

SHE

What a handsome man. Not local, I'll aver.

He comes back.

HE

I met a farmer's labourer some way on;
He says he'll bring them to us here anon,
If possible before the day is dim.
Come down to the inn: there we can wait
for him.

They descend slowly in that direction.

SHE

What a lonely inn. Why is there such a
one?

HE

For us to wait at. Thus 'tis things are
done.

SHE

Thus things are done? Well—what things
do you mean?

HE

Romantic things. Meetings unknown, un-
seen.

SHE

But ours is accident, and needn't have
been,
And isn't what I'd plan with a stranger,
quite,
Particularly at this time—nearly night.

HE

Nor I. But still, the tavern's loneliness
Is favourable for lovers in distress,
When they've eloped, for instance, and are in fear
Of being pursued. No one would find them here.

He goes to speak to the labourer approaching; and returns.

He says the horses long have passed the combe,
And cannot be overtaken. They'll go home.

SHE

And what's to be done? And it's beginning to rain.
'Tis always so. One trouble brings a train!

HE

It seems to me that here we'd better stay
And rest us till some vehicle comes this way:
In fact, we might put up here till the morning:
The floods are high, and night-farers have warning.

SHE

Put up? Do you think so!

HE

I incline to such.
My *dear* (do you mind?)

SHE

Yes.—Well (*more softly*), I don't much,
If I seem like it. But I ought to tell you
One thing. I'm married. Being so, it's well you—

HE

Oh, so am I. (*A silence, he regarding her*)
I note a charming thing—
You stand so stock-still that your ear-ring shakes
At each pulsation which the vein there makes.

SHE

Does it? Perhaps because it's flustering
To be caught thus! (*In a murmur*) Why did we chance to meet here?

HE

God knows! Perhaps to taste a bitter-
sweet here.—
Still, let us enter. Shelter we must get:
The night is darkening and is growing wet.
So, anyhow, you can treat me as a lover
Just for this once. To-morrow 'twill be
over!

They reach the inn. The door is locked, and they discern a board marked "To Let." While they stand stultified a van is seen drawing near with passengers.

SHE

Ah, here's an end of it! The Crewkerne
carrier.

HE

So cynic circumstance erects its barrier!

SHE (*mischievously*)

To your love-making, which would have
grown stronger,
No doubt, if we had stayed on here much
longer?

The carrier comes up. Her companion reluctantly hails him.

HE

Yes. . . . And in which you might have shown some ruth,
Had but the inn been open!—Well, forsooth,
I'm sorry it's not. Are you? Now, dear, the truth!

SHE (*with gentle evasiveness*)

I am—almost. But best 'tis thus to be.
For—dear one—there I've said it!—you can see
That both at one inn (though roomed separately,
Of course)—so lone, too—might have been unfit,
Perfect as 'tis for lovers, I admit.

HE (*after a sigh*)

Carrier! A lift for my wife, please.

SHE (*in quick undertones*)

Wife? But nay—

HE (*continuing*)

Her horse has thrown her and has gone astray:

See she gets safe to Crewkerne. I've to stay.

CARRIER

I will, sir! I'm for Crookhorn straight away.

HE (*to her, aloud*)

Right now, dear. I shall soon be home. Adieu! (*Kisses her*).

SHE (*whispering confusedly*)

You shouldn't! Pretending you are my husband, too!
I now must act the part of wife to you!

HE (*whispering*)

Yes, since I've kissed you, dear. You see it's done
To silence tongues as we're found here alone
At night, by gossipers, and seem as shown
Staying together!

SHE (*whispering*)

Then must I, too, kiss ?

HE

Yes; a mere matter of form you know,
To check all scandal. People will talk so!

SHE

I'd no idea it would reach to this!
(*Kisses him*)
What makes it worse is, I'm ashamed to say,
I've a young baby waiting me at home!

HE

Ah—there you beat me!—But, my dearest, play
The wife to the end, and don't give me away,
Despite the baby, since we've got so far,
And what we've acted feel we almost are!

SHE (*sighing*)

Yes. 'Tis so! And my conscience has gone dumb!

(*Aloud*)

'Bye, dear, awhile! I'll sit up till you come.

(*In a whisper*)

Which means Good-bye for ever, truly heard !
Upon to-night be silent !

HE

Never a word,
Till Pilsdon Pen by Marshwood wind is stirred !

He hands her up. Exeunt omnes.

AT SHAG'S HEATH
1685

(TRADITIONAL)

I GRIEVE and grieve for what I have done,
And nothing now is left to me
But straight to drown; yea, I have slain
The rarest soul the world shall see!
—My husband said: "Now thou art wed
Thou must beware! And should a man
Cajole, mind, he means ill to thee,
Depend on't: fool him if ye can!"
But 'twas King Monmouth, he!

As truth I took what was not true:
Till darked my door just such a one.
He asked me but the way to go,
Though looking all so down and done.
And as he stood he said, unsued,
"The prettiest wife I've eyed to-day!"
And then he kissed me tenderly
Before he footed fast away
Did dear King Monmouth, he!

Builded was he so beautiful!—
Why did I pout a pettish word
For what he'd done?—Then whisking off—
For his pursuers' feet were heard—
"Dear one, keep faith!" he turns and saith,
And next he vanished in the copse
Before I knew what such might be,
And how great fears and how great hopes
Had rare King Monmouth—he!

Up rode the soldiers. "Where's this man?—
He is the rebel Duke," say they.
"And calls himself King Monmouth, sure!"
Then I believed my husband; aye,
Though he'd spoke lies in jealous-wise!
—To Shag's nigh copse beyond the road
I moved my finger mercilessly;
And there lay hidden where I showed:
My dear King Monmouth, he!

The soldiers brought him by my door,
His elbows bound behind him, fast;
Passing, he me-ward cast his eyes—
What eyes of beauty did he cast!
Grieved was his glance at me askance:
"I wished all weal might thee attend,
But this is what th'st done to me,
O heartless woman, held my friend!"
Said sweet King Monmouth, he!

O then I saw he was no hind,
But a great lord of loftihood,
Come here to claim his rule and rights,
Who'd wished me, as he'd said, but good.—
With tug and jolt, then, out to Holt,
To Justice Ettricke, he was led,
And thence to London speedily,
Where under yester's headsman bled
The rare King Monmouth, he!

Last night, the while my husband slept,
He rose up at the window there,
All blood and blear, and hacked about,
With heavy eyes, and rumpled hair;
And said: "My Love, 'twas cruel of
A Fair like thee to use me so!
But now it's nought: from foes I'm free!
Sooner or later all must go,"
Said dear King Monmouth, he!

"Yes, lovely cruel one!" he said
In through the mullioned pane, shroud-pale,
"I love you still, would kiss you now,
But blood would stain your nighty-rail!"
—That's all. And so to drown I go:
O wear no weeds, my friends, for me . . .
When comes the waterman, he'll say,
"Who's done her thuswise?"—'Twill be, yea,
Sweet, slain King Monmouth—he!

A SECOND ATTEMPT

THIRTY years after
I began again
An old-time passion:
And it seemed as fresh as when
The first day ventured on:
When mutely I would waft her
In Love's past fashion
Dreams much dwelt upon,
Dreams I wished she knew.

I went the course through,
From Love's fresh-found sensation—
Remembered still so well—
To worn words charged anew,
That left no more to tell:
Thence to hot hopes and fears,
And thence to consummation,
And thence to sober years,
Markless, and mellow-hued.

Firm the whole fabric stood,
Or seemed to stand, and sound
As it had stood before.
But nothing backward climbs,
And when I looked around
As at the former times,
There was Life—pale and hoar;
And slow it said to me,
"Twice-over cannot be!"

"FREED THE FRET OF THINKING"

FREED the fret of thinking,
  Light of lot were we,
Song with service linking
  Like to bird or bee:
Chancing bale unblinking,
Freed the fret of thinking
  On mortality!

Had not thought-endowment
  Beings ever known,
What Life once or now meant
  None had wanted shown—
Measuring but the moment—
Had not thought-endowment
  Caught Creation's groan!

Loosed from wrings of reason,
  We might blow like flowers,
Sense of Time-wrought treason
  Would not then be ours
In and out of season;
Loosed from wrings of reason
  We should laud the Powers!

THE ABSOLUTE EXPLAINS

I

"ONO," said It: her lifedoings
Time's touch hath not destroyed:
They lie their length, with the throbbing things
Akin them, down the Void,
Live, unalloyed.

II

"Know, Time is toothless, seen all through;
The Present, that men but see,
Is phasmal: since in a sane purview
All things are shaped to be
Eternally.

III

"Your 'Now' is just a gleam, a glide
Across your gazing sense:
With me, 'Past,' 'Future,' ever abide:
They come not, go not, whence
They are never hence.

IV

"As one upon a dark highway,
Plodding by lantern-light,
Finds but the reach of its frail ray
Uncovered to his sight,
Though mid the night.

V

"The road lies all its length the same,
Forwardly as at rear,
So, outside what you 'Present' name,
Future and Past stand sheer,
Cognate and clear."

VI

—Thus It: who straightway opened then
The vista called the Past,
Wherein were seen, as fair as when
They seemed they could not last,
Small things and vast.

VII

There were those songs, a score times sung,
With all their tripping tunes,
There were the laughters once that rung,
There those unmatched full moons,
Those idle noons!

VIII

There fadeless, fixed, were dust-dead flowers
Remaining still in blow;
Elsewhere, wild love-makings in bowers;
Hard by, that irised bow
Of years ago.

IX

There were my ever memorable
Glad days of pilgrimage,
Coiled like a precious parchment fell,
Illumined page by page,
Unhurt by age.

X

"—Here you see spread those mortal ails
So powerless to restrain
Your young life's eager hot assails,
With hazards then not plain
Till past their pain.

XI

"Here you see her who, by these laws
You learn of, still shines on,
As pleasing-pure as erst she was,
Though you think she lies yon,
Graved, glow all gone.

XII

"Here are those others you used to prize.—
But why go further we?
The Future?—Well, I would advise
You let the future be,
Unshown by me!

XIII

" 'Twould harrow you to see undraped
The scenes in ripe array
That wait your globe—all worked and shaped;
And I'll not, as I say,
Bare them to-day.

XIV

"In fine, Time is a mock,—yea, such!—
As he might well confess:
Yet hath he been believed in much,
Though lately, under stress
Of science, less.

XV

"And hence, of her you asked about
At your first speaking: she
Hath, I assure you, not passed out
Of continuity,
But is in me.

XVI

"So thus doth Being's length transcend
Time's ancient regal claim
To see all lengths begin and end.
'The Fourth Dimension' fame
Bruits as its name."

New Year's Eve, 1922.

"SO, TIME"

(*The same thought resumed*)

SO, Time,
Royal, sublime;
Heretofore held to be
Master and enemy,
Thief of my Love's adornings,
Despoiling her to scornings:—
The sound philosopher
Now sets him to aver
You are nought
But a thought
Without reality.

Young, old
Passioned, cold,
All the loved-lost thus
Are beings continuous,
In dateless dure abiding,
Over the present striding
With placid permanence
That knows not transience:
Firm in the Vast,
First, last;
Afar, yet close to us.

AN INQUIRY

A PHANTASY

Circumdederunt me dolores mortis.—Ps. xviii.

I SAID to It: "We grasp not what you meant,
(Dwelling down here, so narrowly pinched and pent)
By crowning Death the King of the Firmament:
—The query I admit to be
One of unwonted size,
But it is put you sorrowingly,
And not in idle-wise."

"Sooth, since you ask me gravely," It replied,
"Though too incisive questions I have decried,
This shows some thought, and may be justified.
I'll gauge its value as I go
Across the Universe,
And bear me back in a moment or so
And say, for better or worse."

Many years later, when It came again,
"That matter an instant back which
brought you pain,"
It said, "and you besought me to explain:
Well, my forethoughtless modes to
you
May seem a shameless thing,
But—I'd no meaning, that I knew,
In crowning Death as King!"

THE FAITHFUL SWALLOW

WHEN summer shone
Its sweetest on
An August day,
"Here evermore,"
I said, "I'll stay;
Not go away
To another shore
As fickle they!"

December came:
'Twas not the same!
I did not know
Fidelity
Would serve me so.
Frost, hunger, snow;
And now, ah me,
Too late to go!

IN SHERBORNE ABBEY

(17—)

THE moon has passed to the panes
of the south-aisle wall,
And brought the mullioned shades and
shines to fall
On the cheeks of a woman and man in
a pew there, pressed
Together as they pant, and recline for
rest.

Forms round them loom, recumbent like
their own,
Yet differing; for they are chiselled in
frigid stone;
In doublets are some; some mailed, as
whilom ahorse they leapt;
And stately husbands and wives, side by
side as they anciently slept.

"We are not like those," she murmurs.
"For ever here set!"
"True, Love," he replies. "We two are
not marble yet."
"And, worse," said she; "not husband
and wife!"
"But we soon shall be" (from him)
"if we've life!"
A silence. A trotting of horses is heard
without.
The lovers scarce breathe till its echo has
quite died out.

"It was they! They have passed, any-
how!"
"Our horse, slily hid by the conduit,
They've missed, or they'd rushed to
impound it!"
"And they'll not discover us now."
"Will not, until 'tis too late,
And we can outface them straight!"

"Why did you make me ride in your front?"
says she.
"To outwit the law. That was my
strategy.
As I was borne off on the pillion behind
you,
Th'abductor was you, Dearest, let me
remind you;

And seizure of me by an heiress is no felony,
Whatever to do it with me as the seizer may be."

Another silence falls. And a cloud comes over the moon:
The print of the panes upon them enfeebles, as fallen in a swoon,
Until they are left in darkness unbroke and profound,
As likewise are left their chill and chiselled neighbours around.

A Family tradition.

THE PAIR HE SAW PASS

O SAD man, now a long dead man,
To whom it was so real,
I picture, as 'twere yesterday,
How you would tell the tale!

Just wived were you, you sad dead man,
And "settling down," you'd say,
And had rigged the house you had reared for yourself
And the mate now yours alway.

You had eyed and tried each door and lock,
And cupboard, and bell, and glass,
When you glanced across to the road without,
And saw a carriage pass.

It bowled along from the old town-gate;
Two forms its freight, and those
Were a just-joined pair, as you discerned
By the favours and the bows.

And one of the pair you saw was a Fair
  Whom you had wooed awhile,
And the other you saw, with a creeping awe,
  Was yourself, in bridegroom style.

"And there we rode as man and wife
  In the broad blaze of the sun,"
Would you aver; yea, you with her
  You had left for another one.

"The morning," you said, my friend long dead,
  "Was ordinary and fine;
And yet there gleamed, it somehow seemed,
  At moments, a strange shine."

You hailed a boy from your garden-plot,
  And sent him along the way
To the parish church; whence word was brought
  No marriage had been that day.

You mused, you said; till you heard anon
  That at that hour she died
Whom once, instead of your living wife,
  You had meant to make your bride. . . .

You, dead man, dwelt in your new-built
house
With no great spirit or will,
And after your soon decease your spouse
Re-mated: she lives there still.

Which should be blamed, if either can,
The teller does not know
For your mismatch, O weird-wed man,
Or what you thought was so.

From an old draft.

THE MOCK WIFE

IT'S a dark drama, this, and yet I know
the house, and date;
That is to say, the where and when John
Channing met his fate.
The house was one in High Street, seen of
burghers still alive.
The year was some two centuries bygone;
seventeen-hundred and five.

And dying was Channing the grocer. All
the clocks had struck eleven,
And the watchers saw that ere the dawn his
soul would be in Heaven;
When he said on a sudden: "I should *like*
to kiss her before I go,—
For one last time!" They looked at each
other and murmured, "Even so."

She'd just been haled to prison, his wife;
yea, charged with shaping his death:
By poison, 'twas told; and now he was
nearing the moment of his last breath:

He, witless that his young housemate was
suspect of such a crime,
Lay thinking that his pangs were but a
malady of the time.

Outside the room they pondered gloomily,
wondering what to do,
As still he craved her kiss—the dying man
who nothing knew:
"Guilty she may not be," they said; "so
why should we torture him
In these his last few minutes of life? Yet
how indulge his whim?"

And as he begged there piteously for what
could not be done,
And the murder-charge had flown about the
town to every one,
The friends around him in their trouble
thought of a hasty plan,
And straightway set about it. Let denounce
them all who can.

"O will you do a kindly deed—it may be
a soul to save;
At least, great misery to a man with one
foot in the grave?"
Thus they to the buxom woman not unlike
his prisoned wife;
"The difference he's past seeing; it will
soothe his sinking life."

Well, the friendly neighbour did it; and he
kissed her; held her fast;
Kissed her again and yet again. "I—knew
she'd—come at last!—
Where have you been?—Ah, kept away!
—I'm sorry—overtried—
God bless you!" And he loosed her, fell
back tiredly, and died.

His wife stood six months after on the
scaffold before the crowd,
Ten thousand of them gathered there; fixed,
silent, and hard-browed,
To see her strangled and burnt to dust, as
was the verdict then
On women truly judged, or false, of doing
to death their men.

Some of them said as they watched her
burn: "I am glad he never knew,
Since a few hold her as innocent—think
such she could not do!
Glad, too, that (as they tell) he thought
she kissed him ere he died."
And they seemed to make no question that
the cheat was justified.

THE FIGHT ON DURNOVER MOOR

(183–)

WE'D loved, we two, some while,
And that had come which comes when men too much beguile;
And without more ado
My lady said: "O shame! Get home, and hide!" But he was true.

Yes: he was true to me,
And helped me some miles homealong; and vowing to come
Before the weeks were three,
And do in church a deed should strike all scandal dumb.

And when we had traipsed to Grey's great Bridge, and pitched my box
On its cope, to breathe us there,
He cried: "What wrangle's that in yonder moor? Those knocks,
Gad, seem not to be fair!

"And a woman on her knees! . . . I'll
go. . . . There's surely something wrong!"
I said: "You are tired and spent
With carrying my heavy things so far and long!"
But he would go, and went.

And there I stood, steadying my box, and screened from none,
Upon the crown of the bridge,
Ashamed o' my shape, as lower and lower slipped the sun
Down behind Pummery Ridge. . . .

"O you may long wait so!
Your young man's done—aye, dead!" they by and by ran and cried.
"You shouldn't have let him go
And join that whorage, but have kept him at your side!

"It was another wench,
Biggening as you, that he championed: yes, he came on straight
With a warmth no words could quench
For her helpless face, as soon as ever he eyed her state,

"And fought her fancy-lad, who had used
her far from well,
So soon to make her moan,
Aye, closed with him in fight, till at a blow
yours fell,
His skull against a stone.

"She'd followed him there, this man who'd
won her, and overwon,
So, when he set to twit her
Yours couldn't abide him—him all other
fighters shun,
For he's a practised hitter.

"Your man moved not, and the constables
came for the other; so he,
He'll never make her his wife
Any more than yours will you; for they
say that at least 'twill be
Across the water for life."

"O what has she brought about!"
I groaned: "this woman met here in my
selfsame plight;
She's put another yielding heart's poor
candle out
By dogging her man to-night!

"He might never have done her his due
Of amends! But mine had bidden the banns for marrying me!
Why did we rest on this bridge; why rush to a quarrel did he
With which he had nothing to do!"

But vain were bursts of blame:
We twain stood like and like, though strangers till that hour,
Foredoomed to tread our paths beneath like gaze and glower,
Bear a like blushful name.

Almost the selfsame day
It fell that her time and mine came on,—a lad and a lass:
The father o' mine was where the worms waggle under the grass,
Of hers, at Botany Bay.

LAST LOOK ROUND ST. MARTIN'S FAIR

THE sun is like an open furnace door,
Whose round revealed retort contains the roar
Of fires beyond terrene;
The moon presents the lustre-lacking face
Of a brass dial gone green,
Whose hours no eye can trace.
The unsold heathcroppers are driven home
To the shades of the Great Forest whence they come
By men with long cord-waistcoats in brown monochrome.
The stars break out, and flicker in the breeze,
It seems, that twitches the trees.—
From its hot idol soon
The fickle unresting earth has turned to a fresh patroon—
The cold, now brighter, moon.

The woman in red, at the nut-stall
with the gun,
Lights up, and still goes on:
She's redder in the flare-lamp than
the sun
Showed it ere it was gone.
Her hands are black with loading all
the day,
And yet she treats her labour as 'twere
play,
Tosses her ear-rings, and talks ribaldry
To the young men around as natural gaiety,
And not a weary work she'd readily
stay,
And never again nut-shooting see,
Though crying, "Fire away!"

THE CARICATURE

OF the Lady Lu there were stories told,
For she was a woman of comely mould,
In heart-experience old.

Too many a man for her whimful sake
Had borne with patience chill and ache,
And nightly lain awake!

This epicure in pangs, in her tooth
For more of the sweet, with a calm unruth
Cast eyes on a painter-youth.

Her junior he; and the bait of bliss
Which she knew to throw—not he to miss—
She threw, till he dreamed her his.

To her arts not blind, he yet sued long,
As a songster jailed by a deed of wrong
Will shower the doer with song;

Till tried by tones now smart, now suave,
He would flee in ire, to return a slave
Who willingly forgave.

When no! One day he left her door,
"I'll ease mine agony!" he swore,
"And bear this thing no more!

"I'll practise a plan!" Thereon he took
Her portrait from his sketching-book,
And, though his pencil shook,

He moulded on the real its mock;
Of beauteous brow, lip, eye, and lock
Composed a laughingstock.

Amazed at this satire of his long lure,
Whenever he scanned it he'd scarce endure
His laughter. 'Twas his cure.

And, even when he woke in the night,
And chanced to think of the comic sight,
He laughed till exhausted quite.

"Why do you laugh?" she said one day
As he gazed at her in a curious way.
"Oh—for nothing," said he. "Mere play."

—A gulf of years then severed the twain;
Till he heard—a painter of high attain—
She was dying on her domain.

"And," dryly added the friend who told,
"You may know or not that, in semblance cold,
She loved once, loved whole-souled;

"And that you were the man? Did you break your vow?
Well, well; she is good as gone by now . . .
But you hit her, all allow!"

Ah, the blow past bearing that he received!
In his bachelor quiet he grieved and grieved;
How cruel; how self-deceived!

Did she ever know?. . . Men pitied his state
As the curse of his own contrivance ate
Like canker into his fate.

For ever that thing of his evil craft
Uprose on his grief—his mocking draught—
Till, racked, he insanely laughed.

Thence onward folk would muse in doubt
What gloomed him so as he walked about,
But few, or none, found out.

A LEADER OF FASHION

NEVER has she known
The way a robin will skip and come,
With an eye half bold, half timorsome,
To the table's edge for a breakfast crumb:

Nor has she seen
A streak of roseate gently drawn
Across the east, that means the dawn,
When, up and out, she foots it on:

Nor has she heard
The rustle of the sparrow's tread
To roost in roof-holes near her head
When dusk bids her, too, seek her bed:

Nor has she watched
Amid a stormy eve's turmoil
The pipkin slowly come to boil,
In readiness for one at toil:

Nor has she hearkened
Through the long night-time, lone and numb,
For sounds of sent-for help to come
Ere the swift-sinking life succumb:

Nor has she ever
Held the loved-lost one on her arm,
Attired with care his straightened form,
As if he were alive and warm:

Yea, never has she
Known, seen, heard, felt, such things as these,
Haps of so many in their degrees
Throughout their count of calvaries!

MIDNIGHT ON BEECHEN, 187–

ON Beechen Cliff self-commune I
This night of mid-June, mute and dry;
When darkness never rises higher
Than Bath's dim concave, towers, and spire,
Last eveglow loitering in the sky

To feel the dawn, close lurking by,
The while the lamps as glow-worms lie
In a glade, myself their lonely eyer
On Beechen Cliff:

The city sleeps below. I sigh,
For there dwells one, all testify,
To match the maddest dream's desire:
What swain with her would not aspire
To walk the world, yea, sit but nigh
On Beechen Cliff!

THE AËROLITE

I THOUGHT a germ of Consciousness
Escaped on an aërolite
Aions ago
From some far globe, where no distress
Had means to mar supreme delight;

But only things abode that made
The power to feel a gift uncloyed
Of gladsome glow,
And life unendingly displayed
Emotions loved, desired, enjoyed.

And that this stray, exotic germ
Fell wanderingly upon our sphere,
After its wingings,
Quickened, and showed to us the worm
That gnaws vitalities native here,

And operated to unblind
Earth's old-established innocence
Of stains and stingings,
Which grin no griefs while not opined
But cruelly tax intelligence.

"How shall we," then the seers said,
"Oust this awareness, this disease
Called sense, here sown,
Though good, no doubt, where it was bred,
And wherein all things work to please?"

Others cried: "Nay, we rather would,
Since this untoward gift is sent
For ends unknown,
Limit its registerings to good,
And hide from it all anguishment."

I left them pondering. This was how
(Or so I dreamed) was waked on earth
The mortal moan
Begot of sentience. Maybe now
Normal unawareness waits rebirth.

THE PROSPECT

THE twigs of the birch imprint the December sky
Like branching veins upon a thin old hand;
I think of summer-time, yes, of last July,
When she was beneath them, greeting a gathered band
Of the urban and bland.

Iced airs wheeze through the skeletoned hedge from the north,
With steady snores, and a numbing that threatens snow,
And skaters pass; and merry boys go forth
To look for slides. But well, well do I know
Whither I would go!

December 1912.

GENITRIX LAESA

(MEASURE OF A SARUM SEQUENCE)

NATURE, through these generations
You have nursed us with a patience
Cruelly crossed by malversations,
Marring mother-ministry
To your multitudes, so blended
By your processes, long-tended,
And the painstaking expended
On their chording tunefully.

But this stuff of slowest moulding,
In your fancy ever enfolding
Life that rhythmic chime is holding:
(Yes; so deem it you, Ladye—
This "concordia discors"!)—truly,
Rather, as if some imp unruly
Twitched your artist-arm when newly
Shaping forth your scenery!

Aye. Yet seem you not to know it.
Hence your world-work needs must show it
Good in dream, in deed below it:
(Lady, yes: so sight it we!)
Thus, then, go on fondly thinking:
Why should man your purblind blinking
Crave to cure, when all is sinking
To dissolubility.

THE FADING ROSE

I SAW a rose, in bloom, but sad,
Shedding the petals that still it had,
And I heard it say: "O where is she
Who used to come and muse on me?

"The pruner says she comes no more
Because she loves another flower,
The weeder says she's tired of me
Because I droop so suddenly.

"Because of a sweetheart she comes not,
Declares the man with the watering-pot;
'She does not come,' says he with the rake,
'Because all women are fickle in make.'

"He with the spade and humorous leer
Says: 'Know, I delve elsewhere than here,
Mid text-writ stones and grassy heaps,
Round which a curious silence creeps.

" 'She must get to you underground
If any way at all be found,
For, clad in her beauty, marble's kin,
'Tis there I have laid her and trod her
in.' "

WHEN OATS WERE REAPED

THAT day when oats were reaped, and
wheat was ripe, and barley ripening,
The road-dust hot, and the bleaching
grasses dry,
I walked along and said,
While looking just ahead to where some
silent people lie:

"I wounded one who's there, and now
know well I wounded her;
But, ah, she does not know that she
wounded me!"
And not an air stirred,
Nor a bill of any bird; and no response
accorded she.

August 1913.

LOUIE

I AM forgetting Louie the buoyant;
Why not raise her phantom, too,
Here in daylight
With the elect one's?
She will never thrust the foremost figure
out of view!

Mid this heat, in gauzy muslin
See I Louie's life-lit brow
Here in daylight
By the elect one's.—
Long two strangers they and far apart;
such neighbours now!

July 1913.

"SHE OPENED THE DOOR"

SHE opened the door of the West to me,
With its loud sea-lashings,
And cliff-side clashings
Of waters rife with revelry.

She opened the door of Romance to me,
The door from a cell
I had known too well,
Too long, till then, and was fain to flee.

She opened the door of a Love to me,
That passed the wry
World-welters by
As far as the arching blue the lea.

She opens the door of the Past to me,
Its magic lights,
Its heavenly heights,
When forward little is to see!

1913.

"WHAT'S THERE TO TELL?"

(SONG)

WHAT'S there to tell of the world
More than is told?
—Into its vortex hurled,
Out of it rolled,
Can we yet more of the world
Find to be told?
Lalla-la, lu!

If some could last alive
Much might be told;
Yes, gladness might survive;
But they go cold—
Each and each late alive—
All their tale told.
Lalla-la, lu!

There's little more of the world,
Then, to be told;

Had ever life unfurled
    Joys manifold
There had been more of the world
    Left to be told.
        Lalla-la, lalla-la, lalla-la, lu!

190–.

THE HARBOUR BRIDGE

FROM here, the quay, one looks above to mark
The bridge across the harbour, hanging dark
Against the day's-end sky, fair-green in glow
Over and under the middle archway's bow:
It draws its skeleton where the sun has set,
Yea, clear from cutwater to parapet;
On which mild glow, too, lines of rope and spar
Trace themselves black as char.

Down here in shade we hear the painters shift
Against the bollards with a drowsy lift,
As moved by the incoming stealthy tide.
High up across the bridge the burghers glide
As cut black-paper portraits hastening on
In conversation none knows what upon:
Their sharp-edged lips move quickly word by word
To speech that is not heard.

There trails the dreamful girl, who leans
and stops,
There presses the practical woman to the
shops,
There is a sailor, meeting his wife with a
start,
And we, drawn nearer, judge they are
keeping apart.
Both pause. She says: "I've looked for
you. I thought
We'd make it up." Then no words can
be caught.
At last: "Won't you come home?" She
moves still nigher:
" 'Tis comfortable, with a fire."

"No," he says gloomily. "And, anyhow,
I can't give up the other woman now:
You should have talked like that in former
days,
When I was last home." They go differ-
ent ways.
And the west dims, and yellow lamplights
shine:
And soon above, like lamps more opaline,
White stars ghost forth, that care not for
men's wives,
Or any other lives.

Weymouth.

VAGRANT'S SONG

(WITH AN OLD WESSEX REFRAIN)

I

WHEN a dark-eyed dawn
Crawls forth, cloud-drawn,
And starlings doubt the night-time's close;
And "three months yet,"
They seem to fret,
"Before we cease us slaves of snows,
And sun returns
To loose the burns,
And this wild woe called Winter goes!"—
O a hollow tree
Is as good for me
As a house where the back-brand glows!
Che-hane, mother; che-hane, mother,
As a house where the back-brand glows!

Line 12: "back-brand"—the log which used to be laid at the back of a wood fire.

II

When autumn brings
A whirr of wings
Among the evergreens around,
And sundry thrills
About their quills
Awe rooks, and misgivings abound,
And the joyless pines
In leaning lines
Protect from gales the lower ground,
O a hollow tree
Is as good for me
As a house of a thousand pound!
Che-hane, mother; che-hane, mother,
As a house of a thousand pound!

FARMER DUNMAN'S FUNERAL

"BURY me on a Sunday,"
He said; "so as to see
Poor folk there. 'Tis their one day
To spare for following me."

And mindful of that Sunday,
He wrote, while he was well,
On ten rum-bottles one day,
"Drink for my funeral."

They buried him on a Sunday,
That folk should not be balked
His wish, as 'twas their one day:
And forty couple walked.

They said: "To have it Sunday
Was always his concern;
His meaning being that one day
He'd do us a good turn.

"We must, had it been Monday,
Have got it over soon,
But now we gain, being Sunday,
A jolly afternoon."

THE SEXTON AT LONGPUDDLE

HE passes down the churchyard track
On his way to toll the bell;
And stops, and looks at the graves around,
And notes each finished and greening mound
Complacently,
As their shaper he,
And one who can do it well.
And, with a prosperous sense of his doing,
Thinks he'll not lack
Plenty such work in the long ensuing
Futurity.
For people will always die,
And he will always be nigh
To shape their cell.

THE HARVEST-SUPPER

(*Circa* 1850)

NELL and the other maids danced their best
With the Scotch-Greys in the barn;
These had been asked to the harvest-feast;
Red shapes amid the corn.

Nell and the other maids sat in a row
Within the benched barn-nook;
Nell led the songs of long ago
She'd learnt from never a book.

She sang of the false Sir John of old,
The lover who witched to win,
And the parrot, and cage of glittering gold;
And the other maids joined in.

Then whispered to her a gallant Grey,
"Dear, sing that ballet again!
For a bonnier mouth in a bonnier way
Has sung not anywhen!"

As she loosed her lips anew there sighed
  To Nell through the dark barn-door
The voice of her Love from the night outside,
  Who was buried the month before:

"O Nell, can you sing ballets there,
  And I out here in the clay,
Of lovers false of yore, nor care
  What you vowed to me one day!

"O can you dance with soldiers bold,
  Who kiss when dancing's done,
Your little waist within their hold,
  As ancient troth were none!"

She cried: "My heart is pierced with a wound!
  There's something outside the wall
That calls me forth to a greening mound:
  I can sing no more at all!

"My old Love rises from the worms,
  Just as he used to be,
And I must let gay gallants' arms
  No more encircle me!"

They bore her home from the merry-
making;
Bad dreams disturbed her bed:
"Nevermore will I dance and sing,"
Mourned Nell; "and never wed!"

AT A PAUSE IN A COUNTRY DANCE

(MIDDLE OF LAST CENTURY)

THEY stood at the foot of the figure,
And panted: they'd danced it down through—
That "Dashing White Serjeant" they loved so:—
A window, uncurtained, was nigh them
That end of the room. Thence in view

Outside it a valley updrew,
Where the frozen moon lit frozen snow:
At the furthermost reach of the valley
A light from a window shone low.
"They are inside that window," said she,

As she looked. "They sit up there for me;
And baby is sleeping there, too."
He glanced. "Yes," he said. "Never mind,"
Let's foot our way up again; do!
And dance down the line as before.

"What's the world to us, meeting once
more!"
"—Not much, when your husband full
trusts you,
And thinks the child his that I bore!"
He was silent. The fiddlers six-eighted
With even more passionate vigour.

The pair swept again up the figure,
The child's cuckoo-father and she,
And the next couples threaded below,
And the twain wove their way to the top
Of "The Dashing White Serjeant" they
loved so,
Restarting: right, left, to and fro.

—From the homestead, seen yon, the small
glow
Still adventured forth over the white,
Where the child slept, unknowing who
sired it,
In the cradle of wicker tucked tight,
And its grandparents, nodding, admired it
In elbow-chairs through the slow night.

ON THE PORTRAIT OF A WOMAN ABOUT TO BE HANGED

COMELY and capable one of our race,
Posing there in your gown of grace,
Plain, yet becoming;
Could subtlest breast
Ever have guessed
What was behind that innocent face,
Drumming, drumming!

Would that your Causer, ere knoll your knell
For this riot of passion, might deign to tell
Why, since It made you
Sound in the germ,
It sent a worm
To madden Its handiwork, when It might well
Not have assayed you,

Not have implanted, to your deep rue,
The Clytaemnestra spirit in you,

And with purblind vision
Sowed a tare
In a field so fair,
And a thing of symmetry, seemly to view,
Brought to derision!

January 6, 1923.

THE CHURCH AND THE WEDDING

"I'LL restore this old church for our marriage:
I've ordered the plans:
Style of wedding your choice—foot or carriage—
By licence, or banns."

He restored it, as though built newly:
The bishop was won
To preach, who pronounced it truly
A thing well done.

But the wedding waits; long, long has waited;
And guesswork is dumb
Why those who were there to have mated
Do not come.

And when the nights moan like the wailings
Of souls sore-tried,
The folk say who pass the church-palings
They hear inside

Strange sounds as of anger and sadness
That cut the heart's core,
And shaken words bitter to madness;
And then no more.

THE SHIVER

FIVE long clangs from the house-clock nigh,
And I woke with a sigh:
Stars wore west like a slow tide flowing,
And my lover had told yesternight of his going,—
That at this gray hour he'd be hasting by,

Starting betimes on a journey afar:—
So, casement ajar,
I eyed in the upland pasture his figure,
A dim dumb speck, growing darker and bigger,
Then smalling to nought where the nut-trees are.

He could not bend his track to my window, he'd said,
Being hurried ahead:
But I wished he had tried to!—and then felt a shiver,

Corpse-cold, as he sank toward the town
by the river;
And back I went sadly and slowly to bed.

What meant my shiver while seeing him
pass
As a dot on the grass
I surmised not then. But later I knew it
When came again he; and my words out-
drew it,
As said he: "It's hard for your bearing,
alas!

"But I've seen, I have clasped, where the
smart ships plough,
One of far brighter brow.
A sea-goddess. Shiver not. One far
rarer
In gifts than I find thee; yea, warmer and
fairer:—
I seek her again; and I love you not now."

"NOT ONLY I"

NOT only I
Am doomed awhile to lie
In this close bin with earthen sides;
But the things I thought, and the songs I sang,
And the hopes I had, and the passioned pang
For people I knew
Who passed before me,
Whose memory barely abides;
And the visions I drew
That daily upbore me!

And the joyous springs and summers,
And the jaunts with blithe newcomers,
And my plans and appearances; drives and rides
That fanned my face to a lively red;
And the grays and blues
Of the far-off views,

That nobody else discerned outspread;
And little achievements for blame or
praise;
Things left undone; things left unsaid;
In brief, my days!

Compressed here in six feet by two,
In secrecy
To lie with me
Till the Call shall be,
Are all these things I knew,
Which cannot be handed on;
Strange happenings quite unrecorded,
Lost to the world and disregarded,
That only thinks: "Here moulders till
Doom's-dawn
A woman's skeleton."

SHE SAW HIM, SHE SAID

"WHY, I saw you with the sexton,
outside the church-door,
So I did not hurry me home,
Thinking you'd not be come,
Having something to him to say.—
Yes: 'twas you, Dear, though you seemed
sad, heart-sore;
How fast you've got therefrom!"

"I've not been out. I've watched the
moon through the birch,
And heard the bell toll. Yes,
Like a passing soul in distress!"
"—But no bell's tolled to-day?" . . .
His face looked strange, like the face of
him seen by the church,
And she sank to musefulness.

ONCE AT SWANAGE

THE spray sprang up across the cusps
of the moon,
And all its light loomed green
As a witch-flame's weirdsome sheen
At the minute of an incantation scene;
And it greened our gaze—that night at
demilune.

Roaring high and roaring low was the sea
Behind the headland shores:
It symboled the slamming of doors,
Or a regiment hurrying over hollow
floors. . . .
And there we two stood, hands clasped;
I and she!

THE FLOWER'S TRAGEDY

IN the bedchamber window, near the glass,
Stood the little flower in the little vase,
Unnoticed quite
For a whole fortnight,
And withered for lack of watering
To a skeleton mere—a mummied thing.

But it was not much, mid a world of teen,
That a flower should waste in a nook unseen!

One needed no thought to ascertain
How it happened; that when she went in the rain
To return here not,
She was mindless what
She had left here to perish.—Ah, well: for an hour
I wished I had not found the flower!

Yet it was not much. And she never had known
Of the flower's fate; nor it of her own.

AT THE AQUATIC SPORTS

WITH their backs to the sea two fiddlers stand
Facing the concourse on the strand,
And a third man who sings.
The sports proceed; there are crab-catchings;
The people laugh as levity spreads;
Yet these three do not turn their heads
To see whence the merriment springs.

They cease their music, but even then
They stand as before, do those three men,
Though pausing, nought to do:
They never face to the seaward view
To enjoy the contests, add their cheer,
So wholly is their being here
A business they pursue.

A WATCHER'S REGRET

J. E.'S STORY

I SLEPT across the front of the clock,
  Close to the long case-door;
The hours were brought by their brazen knock
  To my ear as the slow nights wore.

Thus did I, she being sick to death,
  That each hour as it belled
Should wake me to rise, and learn by her breath
  Whether her strength still held.

Yet though throughout life's midnights all
  I would have watched till spent
For her dear sake, I missed the call
  Of the hour in which she went.

HORSES ABOARD

HORSES in horsecloths stand in a row
On board the huge ship, that at last lets go:
Whither are they sailing? They do not know,
Nor what for, nor how.—
They are horses of war,
And are going to where there is fighting afar;
But they gaze through their eye-holes unwitting they are,
And that in some wilderness, gaunt and ghast,
Their bones will bleach ere a year has passed,
And the item be as "war-waste" classed.—
And when the band booms, and the folk say "Good-bye!"
And the shore slides astern, they appear wrenched awry
From the scheme Nature planned for them,
—wondering why.

THE HISTORY OF AN HOUR

VAIN is the wish to try rhyming it,
writing it!
Pen cannot weld into words what it was;
Time will be squandered in toil at in-
diting it;
Clear is the cause!

Yea, 'twas too satiate with soul, too
ethereal;
June-morning scents of a rose-bush in
flower
Catch in a clap-net of hempen material;
So catch that hour!

THE MISSED TRAIN

HOW I was caught
Hieing home, after days of allure,
And forced to an inn—small, obscure—
At the junction, gloom-fraught.

How civil my face
To get them to chamber me there—
A roof I had scorned, scarce aware
That it stood at the place.

And how all the night
I had dreams of the unwitting cause
Of my lodgment. How lonely I was;
How consoled by her sprite!

Thus onetime to me . . .
Dim wastes of dead years bar away
Then from now. But such happenings to-day
Fall to lovers, may be!

Years, years as shoaled seas,
Truly, stretch now between! Less and less
Shrink the visions then vast in me.—Yes,
Then in me: Now in these.

UNDER HIGH-STOY HILL

FOUR climbed High-Stoy from Ivel-
wards,
Where hedge meets hedge, and cart-ruts
wind,
Chattering like birds,
And knowing not what lay behind.

We laughed beneath the moonlight blink,
Said supper would be to our mind,
And did not think
Of Time, and what might lie behind. . . .

The moon still meets that tree-tipped
height,
The road—as then—still trails inclined;
But since that night
We have well learnt what lay behind!

For all of the four then climbing here
But one are ghosts, and he brow-lined;
With him they fare,
Yet speak not of what lies behind.

AT THE MILL

O MILLER KNOX, whom we knew
well,
And the mill, and the floury floors,
And the corn,—and those two women,
And infants—yours!

The sun was shining when you rode
To market on that day:
The sun was set when home-along
You ambled in the gray,
And gathered what had taken place
While you were away.

O Miller Knox, 'twas grief to see
Your good wife hanging there
By her own rash and passionate hand,
In a throe of despair;

And those two children, one by her,
And one by the waiting-maid,
Borne the same hour, and you afar,
And she past aid.

And though sometimes you walk of nights,
  Sleepless, to Yalbury Brow,
And glance the graveyard way, and grunt,
  "'Twas not much, anyhow:
She shouldn't ha' minded!" nought it
    helps
    To say that now.

And the water dribbles down your wheel,
  Your mead blooms green and gold,
And birds twit in your apple-boughs
    Just as of old.

ALIKE AND UNLIKE

(GREAT-ORME'S HEAD)

WE watched the selfsame scene on that long drive,
Saw the magnificent purples, as one eye,
Of those near mountains; saw the storm arrive;
Laid up the sight in memory, you and I,
As if for joint recallings by and by.

But our eye-records, like in hue and line,
Had superimposed on them, that very day,
Gravings on your side deep, but slight on mine!—
Tending to sever us thenceforth alway;
Mine commonplace; yours tragic, gruesome, gray.

THE THING UNPLANNED

THE white winter sun struck its stroke on the bridge,
The meadow-rills rippled and gleamed
As I left the thatched post-office, just by the ridge,
And dropped in my pocket her long tender letter,
With: "This must be snapped! it is more than it seemed;
And now is the opportune time!"

But against what I willed worked the surging sublime
Of the thing that I did—the thing better!

THE SHEEP BOY

A YAWNING, sunned concave
Of purple, spread as an ocean wave
Entroughed on a morning of swell and sway
After a night when wind-fiends have been heard to rave:
Thus was the Heath called "Draäts", on an August day.

Suddenly there intunes a hum:
This side, that side, it seems to come.
From the purple in myriads rise the bees
With consternation mid their rapt employ.
So headstrongly each speeds him past, and flees,
As to strike the face of the shepherd-boy.

Awhile he waits, and wonders what they mean;
Till none is left upon the shagged demesne.

To learn what ails, the sheep-boy looks around;
Behind him, out of the sea in swirls
Flexuous and solid, clammy vapour-curls
Are rolling over Pokeswell Hills to the inland ground.
Into the heath they sail,
And travel up the vale
Like the moving pillar of cloud raised by the Israelite:—
In a trice the lonely sheep-boy seen so late ago,
Draäts'-Hollow in gorgeous blow,
And Kite-Hill's regal glow,
Are viewless—folded into those creeping scrolls of white.

On Rainbarrows.

RETTY'S PHASES

I

RETTY used to shake her head,
  Look with wicked eye;
Say, "I'd tease you, simplehead,
  If I cared to try!"
Then she'd hot-up scarlet red,
  Stilly step away,
Much afraid that what she'd said
  Sounded bold to say.

II

Retty used to think she loved
  (Just a little) me
Not untruly, as it proved
  Afterwards to be.
For, when weakness forced her rest
  If we walked a mile,
She would whisper she was blest
  By my clasp awhile.

III

Retty used at last to say
  When she neared the Vale,
"Mind that you, Dear, on that day
  Ring my wedding peal!"
And we all, with pulsing pride,
  Vigorous sounding gave
Those six bells, the while outside
  John filled in her grave.

IV

Retty used to draw me down
  To the turfy heaps,
Where, with yeoman, squire, and clown
  Noticeless she sleeps.
Now her silent slumber-place
  Seldom do I know,
For when last I saw her face
  Was so long ago!

From an old draft of 1868.

NOTE.—In many villages it was customary after the funeral of an unmarried young woman to ring a peal as for her wedding while the grave was being filled in, as if Death were not to be allowed to balk her of bridal honours. Young unmarried men were always her bearers.

A POOR MAN AND A LADY

WE knew it was not a valid thing,
And only sanct in the sight of God
(To use your phrase), as with fervent nod
You swore your assent when I placed the ring
On your pale slim hand. Our whispering
Was soft as the fan of a turtledove
That round our heads might have seemed to wing;
So solemn were we; so sincere our love.

We could do no better; and thus it stood
Through a time of timorous secret bliss,
Till we were divided, and never a kiss
Of mine could touch you, or likelihood
Illumed our sky that we might, or should
Be each to each in the world's wide eye
What we were unviewed; and our vows make good
In the presence of parents and standers by.

I was a striver with deeds to do,
And little enough to do them with,
And a comely woman of noble kith,
With a courtly match to make, were you;
And we both were young; and though sterling-true
You had proved to our pledge under previous strains,
Our "union," as we called it, grew
Less grave to your eyes in your town campaigns.

Well: the woeful neared, you needn't be told:
The current news-sheets clarioned soon
That you would be wived on a summer noon
By a man of illustrious line and old:
Nor better nor worse than the manifold
Of marriages made, had there not been
Our faith-swearing when fervent-souled,
Which, to me, seemed a breachless bar between.

We met in a Mayfair church, alone:
(The request was mine, which you yielded to.)
"But we were not married at all!" urged you:
"Why, of course we were!" I said. Your tone,

I noted, was world-wise. You went on:
" 'Twas sweet while it lasted. But you
well know
That law is law. He'll be, anon,
My husband *really*. You, Dear, weren't
so."

"I wished—but to learn if——" faltered
I,
And stopped. "But I'll sting you not.
Farewell!"
And we parted.—Do you recall the bell
That tolled by chance as we said good-
bye? . . .
I saw you no more. The track of a high,
Sweet, liberal lady you've doubtless trod.
—All's past! No heart was burst thereby,
And no one knew, unless it was God.

NOTE.—The foregoing was intended to preserve an episode in the story of "The Poor Man and the Lady," written in 1868, and, like these lines, in the first person; but never printed, and ultimately destroyed.

AN EXPOSTULATION

WHY want to go afar
Where pitfalls are,
When all we swains adore
Your featness more and more
As heroine of our artless masquings here,
And count few Wessex' daughters half so dear?

Why paint your appealing face,
When its born grace
Is such no skill can match
With powder, puff, or patch,
Whose every touch defames your bloomfulness,
And with each stain increases our distress?

Yea, is it not enough
That (rare or rough
Your lines here) all uphold you,
And as with wings enfold you,
But you must needs desert the kine-cropt vale
Wherein your foredames gaily filled the pail?

TO A SEA-CLIFF

(DURLSTON HEAD)

LEND me an ear
While I read you here
A page from your history,
Old cliff—not known
To your solid stone,
Yet yours inseparably.

Near to your crown
There once sat down
A silent listless pair;
And the sunset ended,
And dark descended,
And still the twain sat there.

Past your jutting head
Then a line-ship sped,
Lit brightly as a city;
And she sobbed: "There goes
A man who knows
I am his, beyond God's pity!"

He slid apart
Who had thought her heart
His own, and not aboard
A bark, sea-bound. . . .
That night they found
Between them lay a sword.

THE ECHO ELF ANSWERS

HOW much shall I love her?
For life, or not long?
"Not long."

Alas! When forget her?
In years, or by June?
"By June."

And whom woo I after?
No one, or a throng?
"A throng."

Of these shall I wed one
Long hence, or quite soon?
"Quite soon."

And which will my bride be?
The right or the wrong?
"The wrong."

And my remedy—what kind?
Wealth-wove, or earth-hewn?
"Earth-hewn."

CYNIC'S EPITAPH

A RACE with the sun as he downed
I ran at evetide,
Intent who should first gain the ground
And there hide.

He beat me by some minutes then,
But I triumphed anon,
For when he'd to rise up again
I stayed on.

A BEAUTY'S SOLILOQUY DURING HER HONEYMOON

TOO late, too late! I did not know my fairness
Would catch the world's keen eyes so!
How the men look at me! My radiant rareness
I deemed not they would prize so!

That I was a peach for any man's possession
Why did not some one say
Before I leased myself in an hour's obsession
To this dull mate for aye!

His days are mine. I am one who cannot steal her
Ahead of his plodding pace:
As he is, so am I. One doomed to feel her
A wasted form and face!

I was so blind! It did sometimes just strike me
All girls were not as I,
But, dwelling much alone, how few were like me
I could not well descry;

Till, at this Grand Hotel, all looks bend on me
In homage as I pass
To take my seat at breakfast, dinner,—con me
As poorly spoused, alas!

I was too young. I dwelt too much on duty:
If I had guessed my powers
Where might have sailed this cargo of choice beauty
In its unanchored hours!

Well, husband, poor plain man; I've lost life's battle!—
Come—let them look at me.
O damn, don't show in your looks that I'm your chattel
Quite so emphatically!

In a London Hotel, 1892.

DONAGHADEE

(SONG)

I'VE never gone to Donaghadee,
That vague far townlet by the sea;
In Donaghadee I shall never be:
Then why do I sing of Donaghadee,
That I know not in a faint degree? . . .
—Well, once a woman wrote to me
With a tender pen from Donaghadee.

"Susan," I've sung, "Pride of Kildare,"
Because I'd heard of a Susan there,
The "Irish Washerwoman's" capers
I've shared for hours to midnight tapers,
And "Kitty O'Linch" has made me spin
Till dust rose high, and day broke in:
That other "Kitty, of Coleraine,"
Too, set me aching in heart and brain:
While "Kathleen Mavourneen," of course,
would ring
When that girl learnt to make me sing.

Then there was "Irish Molly O"
I tuned as "the fairest one I know,"
And "Nancy Dawson," if I remember,
Rhymed sweet in moonlight one September.

But the damsel who once wrote so free
And tender toned from Donaghadee,
Is a woman who has no name for me—
Moving sylph-like, mysteriously,
(For doubtless, of that sort is she)
In the pathways of her destiny;
But that is where I never shall be;—
And yet I sing of Donaghadee!

HE INADVERTENTLY CURES HIS LOVE-PAINS

(SONG)

I SAID: "O let me sing the praise
Of her who sweetly racks my days,—
Her I adore;
Her lips, her eyes, her moods, her ways!"

In miseries of pulse and pang
I strung my harp, and straightway sang
As none before:—
To wondrous words my quavers rang!

Thus I let heartaches lilt my verse,
Which suaged and soothed, and made disperse
The smarts I bore
To quiet like a sepulchre's.

But, eased, the days that thrilled ere then
Lost value; and I ask, O when,
And how, restore
Those old sweet agonies again!

THE PEACH PEAL

(AFTER FOUR YEARS OF SILENCE)

SAID a wistful daw in Saint Peter's tower,
High above Casterbridge slates and tiles,
Why do the walls of my Gothic bower
Shiver, and shrill out sounds for miles?
This gray old rubble
Has scorned such din
Since I knew trouble
And joy herein.
How still did abide them
These bells now swung,
While our nest beside them
Securely clung! . . .
It means some snare
For our feet or wings;
But I'll be ware
Of such baleful things!"
And forth he flew from his louvred niche
To take up life in a damp dark ditch.

—So mortal motives are misread,
And false designs attributed,
In upper spheres of straws and sticks,
Or lower, of pens and politics.

At the end of the War.

LADY VI

THERE goes the Lady Vi. How well,
How well I know the spectacle
The earth presents
And its events
To her sweet sight
Each day and night!

"Life is a wheeling show, with *me*
As its pivot of interest constantly.
Below in the hollows of towns is sin,
Like a blue brimstone mist therein,
Which makes men lively who plunge amid it,
But wrongfully, and wives forbid it.
London is a place for prancing
Along the Row and, later, dancing
Till dawn, with tightening arm-elbowments
As hours warm up to tender moments.

Travel is piquant, and most thrilling
If, further, joined to big-game killing:
At home, too, hunting, hounds full cry,
When Reynard nears his time to die,
'Tis glee to mark his figure flag,
And how his brush begins to drag,
Till, his earth reached by many a wend,
He finds it *stopped,* and meets his end.

"Religion is good for all who are meek;
It stays in the Bible through the week,
And floats about the house on Sundays,
But does not linger on till Mondays.
The ten Commandments in one's prime
Are matter for another time,
While griefs and graves and things allied
In well-bred talk one keeps outside."

A POPULAR PERSONAGE AT HOME

"I LIVE here: 'Wessex' is my name:
I am a dog known rather well:
I guard the house; but how that came
To be my whim I cannot tell.

"With a leap and a heart elate I go
At the end of an hour's expectancy
To take a walk of a mile or so
With the folk I let live here with me.

"Along the path, amid the grass
I sniff, and find out rarest smells
For rolling over as I pass
The open fields towards the dells.

"No doubt I shall always cross this sill,
And turn the corner, and stand steady,
Gazing back for my mistress till
She reaches where I have run already,

"And that this meadow with its brook,
And bulrush, even as it appears
As I plunge by with hasty look,
Will stay the same a thousand years."

Thus "Wessex." But a dubious ray
At times informs his steadfast eye,
Just for a trice, as though to say,
"Yet, will this pass, and pass shall I?"

1924.

INSCRIPTIONS FOR A PEAL OF EIGHT BELLS

AFTER A RESTORATION

I. THOMAS TREMBLE new-made me
Eighteen hundred and fifty-three:
Why he did I fail to see.

II. I was well-toned by William Brine,
Seventeen hundred and twenty-nine;
Now, re-cast, I weakly whine!

III. Fifteen hundred used to be
My date, but since they melted me
'Tis only eighteen fifty-three.

IV. Henry Hopkins got me made,
And I summon folk as bade;
Not to much purpose, I'm afraid!

V. I likewise; for I bang and bid
In commoner metal than I did,
Some of me being stolen and hid.

VI. I, too, since in a mould they flung me,
Drained my silver, and rehung me,
So that in tin-like tones I tongue me.

VII. In nineteen hundred, so 'tis said,
They cut my canon off my head,
And made me look scalped, scraped,
and dead.

VIII. I'm the peal's tenor still, but rue it!
Once it took two to swing me
through it:
Now I'm rehung, one dolt can do it.

A REFUSAL

SAID the grave Dean of Westminster:
Mine is the best minster
Seen in Great Britain,
As many have written:
So therefore I cannot
Rule here if I ban not
Such liberty-taking
As movements for making
Its greyness environ
The memory of Byron,
Which some are demanding
Who think them of standing,
But in my own viewing
Require some subduing
For tendering suggestions
On Abbey-wall questions
That must interfere here
With my proper sphere here,
And bring to disaster
This fane and its master,
Whose dict is but Christian
Though nicknamed Philistian.

A lax Christian charity—
No mental clarity
Ruling its movements
For fabric improvements—
Demands admonition
And strict supervision
When bent on enshrining
Rapscallions, and signing
Their names on God's stonework,
As if like His own work
Were their lucubrations:
And passed is my patience
That such a creed-scorner
(Not mentioning horner)
Should claim Poet's Corner.

'Tis urged that some sinners
Are here for worms' dinners
Already in person;
That he could not worsen
The walls by a name mere
With men of such fame here.
Yet nay; they but leaven
The others in heaven
In just true proportion,
While more mean distortion.

'Twill next be expected
That I get erected
To Shelley a tablet

In some niche or gablet.
Then—what makes my skin burn,
Yea, forehead to chin burn—
That I ensconce Swinburne!

August 1924.

EPITAPH ON A PESSIMIST

I'M Smith of Stoke, aged sixty-odd,
I've lived without a dame
From youth-time on; and would to God
My dad had done the same.

From the French.

THE PROTEAN MAIDEN

(SONG)

THIS single girl is two girls:
  How strange such things should be!
One noon eclipsed by few girls,
  The next no beauty she.

And daily cries the lover,
  In voice and feature vext:
"My last impression of her
  Is never to be the next!

"She's plain: I will forget her!
  She's turned to fair. Ah no,
Forget?—not I! I'll pet her
  With kisses swift and slow."

A WATERING-PLACE LADY INVENTORIED

A SWEETNESS of temper unsurpassed and unforgettable,
A mole on the cheek whose absence would have been regrettable,
A ripple of pleasant converse full of modulation,
A bearing of inconveniences without vexation,
Till a cynic would find her amiability provoking,
Tempting him to indulge in mean and wicked joking.

Flawlessly oval of face, especially cheek and chin,
With a glance of a quality that beckoned for a glance akin,
A habit of swift assent to any intelligence broken,
Before the fact to be conveyed was fully spoken

And she could know to what her colloquist
would win her,—
This from a too alive impulsion to sympathy in her,—
All with a sense of the ridiculous, keen yet charitable;
In brief, a rich, profuse attractiveness unnarratable.

I should have added her hints that her husband prized her but slenderly,
And that (with a sigh) 'twas a pity she'd no one to treat her tenderly.

THE ROVER COME HOME

HE'S journeyed through America
From Canso Cape to Horn,
And from East Indian Comorin
To Behring's Strait forlorn;
He's felled trees in the backwoods,
In swamps has gasped for breath;
In Tropic heats, in Polar ice,
Has often prayed for death.

He has fought and bled in civil wars
Of no concern to him,
Has shot his fellows—beasts and men—
At risk of life and limb.
He has suffered fluxes, fevers,
Agues, and ills allied,
And now he's home. You look at him
As he talks by your fireside.

And what is written in his glance
Stressed by such foreign wear,
After such alien circumstance
What does his face declare?

His mother's; she who saw him not
  After his starting year,
Who never left her native spot,
  And lies in the churchyard near.

"KNOWN HAD I"

(SONG)

KNOWN had I what I knew not
When we met eye to eye,
That thenceforth I should view not
Again beneath the sky
So truefooted a farer
As you who faced me then,
My path had been a rarer
Than it figures among men!

I would have trod beside you
To guard your feet all day,
And borne at night to guide you
A lantern on your way:
Would not have left you lonely
With wringing doubt, to cow
Old hope, if I could only
Have known what I know now.

THE PAT OF BUTTER

ONCE, at the Agricultural Show,
We tasted—all so yellow—
Those butter-pats, cool and mellow!
Each taste I still remember, though
It was so long ago.

This spoke of the grass of Netherhay,
And this of Kingcomb Hill,
And this of Coker Rill:
Which was the prime I could not say
Of all those tried that day,

Till she, the fair and wicked-eyed,
Held out a pat to me:
Then felt I all Yeo-Lea
Was by her sample sheer outvied;
And, "This is the best," I cried.

BAGS OF MEAT

"HERE'S a fine bag of meat,"
Says the master-auctioneer,
As the timid, quivering steer,
Starting a couple of feet
At the prod of a drover's stick,
And trotting lightly and quick,
A ticket stuck on his rump,
Enters with a bewildered jump.

"Where he's lived lately, friends,
I'd live till lifetime ends:
They've a whole life everyday
Down there in the Vale, have they!
He'd be worth the money to kill
And give away Christmas for good-will."

"Now here's a heifer—worth more
Than bid, were she bone-poor;
Yet she's round as a barrel of beer";
"She's a plum," said the second auctioneer.

"Now this young bull—for thirty pound?
Worth that to manure your ground!"
"Or to stand," chimed the second one,
"And have his picter done!"
The beast was rapped on the horns and snout
To make him turn about.
"Well," cried a buyer, "another crown—
Since I've dragged here from Taunton Town!"

"That calf, she sucked three cows,
Which is not matched for bouse
In the nurseries of high life
By the first-born of a nobleman's wife!"
The stick falls, meaning, "A true tale's told,"
On the buttock of the creature sold,
And the buyer leans over and snips
His mark on one of the animal's hips.

Each beast, when driven in,
Looks round at the ring of bidders there
With a much-amazed reproachful stare,
As at unnatural kin,
For bringing him to a sinister scene
So strange, unhomelike, hungry, mean;
His fate the while suspended between

A butcher, to kill out of hand,
And a farmer, to keep on the land;
One can fancy a tear runs down his face
When the butcher wins, and he's driven
from the place.

THE SUNDIAL ON A WET DAY

I DRIP, drip here
In Atlantic rain,
Falling like handfuls
Of winnowed grain,
Which, tear-like, down
My gnomon drain,
And dim my numerals
With their stain,—
Till I feel useless,
And wrought in vain!

And then I think
In my despair
That, though unseen,
He is still up there,
And may gaze out
Anywhen, anywhere;
Not to help clockmen
Quiz and compare,
But in kindness to let me
My trade declare.

St. Juliot.

HER HAUNTING-GROUND

CAN it be so? It must be so,
That visions have not ceased to be
In this the chiefest sanctuary
Of her whose form we used to know.
—Nay, but her dust is far away,
And "where her dust is, shapes her shade,
If spirit clings to flesh," they say:
Yet here her life-parts most were played!

Her voice explored this atmosphere,
Her foot impressed this turf around,
Her shadow swept this slope and mound,
Her fingers fondled blossoms here;
And so, I ask, why, why should she
Haunt elsewhere, by a slighted tomb,
When here she flourished sorrow-free,
And, save for others, knew no gloom?

A PARTING-SCENE

THE two pale women cried,
But the man seemed to suffer more,
Which he strove hard to hide.
They stayed in the waiting-room, behind the door,
Till startled by the entering engine-roar,
As if they could not bear to have unfurled
Their misery to the eyes of all the world.

A soldier and his young wife
Were the couple; his mother the third,
Who had seen the seams of life.
He was sailing for the East I later heard.
—They kissed long, but they did not speak a word;
Then, strained, he went. To the elder the wife in tears
"Too long; too long!" burst out. ('Twas for five years.)

SHORTENING DAYS AT THE HOMESTEAD

THE first fire since the summer is lit,
and is smoking into the room:
The sun-rays thread it through, like woof-lines in a loom.
Sparrows spurt from the hedge, whom misgivings appal
That winter did not leave last year for ever, after all.
Like shock-headed urchins, spiny-haired,
Stand pollard willows, their twigs just bared.

Who is this coming with pondering pace,
Black and ruddy, with white embossed,
His eyes being black, and ruddy his face,
And the marge of his hair like morning frost?

It's the cider-maker,
And appletree-shaker,
And behind him on wheels, in readi-
ness,
His mill, and tubs, and vat, and press.

DAYS TO RECOLLECT

DO you recall
That day in Fall
When we walked towards Saint Alban's
Head,
Over thistledown that summer had shed,
Or must I remind you?
Winged thistle-seeds which hitherto
Had lain as none were there, or few,
But rose at the brush of your petticoat-seam
(As ghosts might rise of the recent dead),
And sailed on the breeze in a nebulous
stream
Like a comet's tail behind you:
You don't recall
That day in Fall?

Then do you remember
That sad November
When you left me never to see me more,
And looked quite other than theretofore,
As if it could not *be* you?

And lay by the window whence you had
gazed
So many times when blamed or praised,
Morning or noon, through years and years,
Accepting the gifts that Fortune bore,
Sharing, enduring, joys, hopes, fears!
Well: I never more did see you.—
Say you remember
That sad November!

TO C. F. H.

ON HER CHRISTENING-DAY

FAIR Caroline, I wonder what
You think of earth as a dwelling-spot,
And if you'd rather have come, or not?

To-day has laid on you a name
That, though unasked for, you will claim
Lifelong, for love or praise or blame.

May chance and change impose on you
No heavier burthen than this new
Care-chosen one your future through!

Dear stranger here, the prayer is mine
That your experience may combine
Good things with glad. . . . Yes, Caroline!

THE HIGH-SCHOOL LAWN

GRAY prinked with rose,
White tipped with blue,
Shoes with gay hose,
Sleeves of chrome hue;
Fluffed frills of white,
Dark bordered light;
Such shimmerings through
Trees of emerald green are eyed
This afternoon, from the road outside.

They whirl around:
Many laughters run
With a cascade's sound;
Then a mere one.

A bell: they flee:
Silence then:—
So it will be
Some day again
With them,—with me.

THE FORBIDDEN BANNS

A BALLAD OF THE EIGHTEEN-THIRTIES

I

"O WHAT'S the gain, my worthy Sir,
In stopping the banns to-day!
Your son declares he'll marry her
If a thousand folk say Nay."

"I'll do't; I'll do't; whether or no!
And, if I drop down dead,
To church this morning I will go,
And say they shall not wed!"

That day the parson clear outspoke
The maid's name and the man's:
His father, mid the assembled folk
Said, "I forbid the banns!"

Then, white in face, lips pale and cold,
He turned him to sit down,
When he fell forward; and behold,
They found his life had flown.

II

'Twas night-time, towards the middle part,
  When low her husband said,
"I would from the bottom of my heart
  That father was not dead!"

She turned from one to the other side,
  And a sad woman was she
As he went on: "He'd not have died
  Had it not been for me!"

She brought him soon an idiot child,
  And then she brought another:
His face waned wan, his manner wild
  With hatred of their mother.

"Hearken to me, my son. No: no:
  There's madness in her blood!"
Those were his father's words; and lo,
  Now, now he understood.

What noise is that? One noise, and two
  Resound from a near gun.
Two corpses found: and neighbours knew
  By whom the deed was done.

THE PAPHIAN BALL

ANOTHER CHRISTMAS EXPERIENCE OF THE MELLSTOCK QUIRE

WE went our Christmas rounds once more,
With quire and viols as theretofore.

Our path was near by Rushy-Pond,
Where Egdon-Heath outstretched beyond.

There stood a figure against the moon,
Tall, spare, and humming a weirdsome tune.

"You tire of Christian carols," he said:
"Come and lute at a ball instead.

" 'Tis to your gain, for it ensures
That many guineas will be yours.

"A slight condition hangs on't, true,
But you will scarce say nay thereto:

"That you go blindfold; that anon
The place may not be gossiped on."

They stood and argued with each other:
"Why sing from one house to another

"These ancient hymns in the freezing night,
And all for nought? 'Tis foolish, quite!"

"—'Tis serving God, and shunning evil:
Might not elsedoing serve the devil?"

"But grand pay!" . . . They were lured by his call,
Agreeing to go blindfold all.

They walked, he guiding, some new track,
Doubting to find the pathway back.

In a strange hall they found them when
They were unblinded all again.

Gilded alcoves, great chandeliers,
Voluptuous paintings ranged in tiers.

In brief, a mansion large and rare,
With rows of dancers waiting there.

They tuned and played; the couples danced;
Half-naked women tripped, advanced,

With handsome partners footing fast,
Who swore strange oaths, and whirled them past.

And thus and thus the slow hours wore them:
While shone their guineas heaped before them.

Drowsy at length, in lieu of the dance
"*While Shepherds watched* . . ." they bowed by chance;

And in a moment, at a blink,
There flashed a change; ere they could think

The ball-room vanished and all its crew:
Only the well-known heath they view—

The spot of their crossing overnight,
When wheedled by the stranger's sleight.

There, east, the Christmas dawn hung red,
And dark Rainbarrow with its dead

Bulged like a supine negress' breast
Against Clyffe-Clump's faint far-off crest.

Yea; the rare mansion, gorgeous, bright,
The ladies, gallants, gone were quite.

The heaped-up guineas, too, were gone
With the gold table they were on.

"Why did not grasp we what was owed!"
Cried some, as homeward, shamed, they strode.

Now comes the marvel and the warning:
When they had dragged to church next morning,

With downcast heads and scarce a word,
They were astound at what they heard.

Praises from all came forth in showers
For how they'd cheered the midnight hours.

"We've heard you many times," friends said,
"But like *that* never have you played!

"Rejoice ye tenants of the earth,
And celebrate your Saviour's birth,

"Never so thrilled the darkness through,
Or more inspired us so to do!" . . .

—The man who used to tell this tale
Was the tenor-viol, Michael Mail;

Yes; Mail the tenor, now but earth!—
I give it for what it may be worth.

ON MARTOCK MOOR

I

MY deep-dyed husband trusts me,
He feels his mastery sure,
Although I leave his evening hearth
To walk upon the moor.

II

—I had what wealth I needed,
And of gay gowns a score,
And yet I left my husband's house
To muse upon the moor.

III

O how I loved a dear one
Who, save in soul, was poor!
O how I loved the man who met
Me nightly on the moor.

IV

I'd feather-beds and couches,
  And carpets for the floor,
Yet brighter to me was, at eves,
  The bareness of the moor.

V

There was a dogging figure,
  There was a hiss of "Whore!"
There was a flounce at Weir-water
  One night upon the moor. . . .

VI

Yet do I haunt there, knowing
  By rote each rill's low pour,
But only a fitful phantom now
  Meets me upon the moor.

1899.

THAT MOMENT

THE tragedy of that moment
Was deeper than the sea,
When I came in that moment
And heard you speak to me!

What I could not help seeing
Covered life as a blot;
Yes, that which I was seeing,
And knew that you were not!

PREMONITIONS

"THE bell went heavy to-day
At afternoon service, they say,
And a screech-owl cried in the boughs,
And a raven flew over the house,
And Betty's old clock with one hand,
That's worn out, as I understand,
And never goes now, never will,
Struck twelve when the night was dead
still,
Just as when my last loss came to me. . . .
Ah! I wonder who next it will be!

THIS SUMMER AND LAST

UNHAPPY summer you,
Who do not see
What your yester-summer saw!
Never, never will you be
Its match to me,
Never, never draw
Smiles your forerunner drew,
Know what it knew!

Divine things done and said
Illumined it,
Whose rays crept into corn-brown curls,
Whose breezes heard a humorous wit
Of fancy flit.—
Still the alert brook purls,
Though feet that there would tread
Elsewhere have sped.

So, bran-new summer, you
Will never see
All that yester-summer saw!

Never, never will you be
In memory
Its rival, never draw
Smiles your forerunner drew,
Know what it knew!

1913?

"NOTHING MATTERS MUCH"

(B. F. L.)

"NOTHING matters much," he said
Of something just befallen unduly:
He, then active, but now dead,
Truly, truly!

He knew the letter of the law
As voiced by those of wig and gown,
Whose slightest syllogistic flaw
He hammered down.

And often would he shape in word
That nothing needed much lamenting;
And she who sat there smiled and heard,
Sadly assenting.

Facing the North Sea now he lies,
Toward the red altar of the East,
The Flamborough roar his psalmodies,
The wind his priest.

And while I think of his bleak bed,
Of Time that builds, of Time that shatters,
Lost to all thought is he, who said
"Nothing much matters."

IN THE EVENING

IN MEMORIAM FREDERICI TREVES, 1853–1923
(*Dorchester Cemetery, Jan.* 2, 1924)

IN the evening, when the world knew he was dead,
He lay amid the dust and hoar
Of ages; and to a spirit attending said:
"This chalky bed?—
I surely seem to have been here before?"

"O yes. You have been here. You knew the place,
Substanced as you, long ere your call:
And if you cared to do so you might trace
In this gray space
Your being, and the being of men all."

Thereto said he: "Then why was I called away?
I knew no trouble or discontent:
Why did I not prolong my ancient stay
Herein for aye?"
The spirit shook its head. "None knows: you went.

"And though, perhaps, Time did not sign
to you
The need to go, dream-vision sees
How Aesculapius' phantom hither flew,
With Galen's, too,
And his of Cos—plague-proof Hippocrates,

"And beckoned you forth, whose skill had
read as theirs,
Maybe, had Science chanced to spell
In their day, modern modes to stem despairs
That mankind bears! . . .
Enough. You have returned. And all is
well."

THE SIX BOARDS

SIX boards belong to me:
I do not know where they may be;
If growing green, or lying dry
In a cockloft nigh.

Some morning I shall claim them,
And who may then possess will aim them
To bring to me those boards I need
With thoughtful speed.

But though they hurry so
To yield me mine, I shall not know
How well my want they'll have supplied
When notified.

Those boards and I—how much
In common we, of feel and touch
Shall share thence on,—earth's far core-quakings,
Hill-shocks, tide-shakings—

Yea, hid where none will note,
The once live tree and man, remote
From mundane hurt as if on Venus, Mars,
Or furthest stars.

BEFORE MY FRIEND ARRIVED

I SAT on the eve-lit weir,
Which gurgled in sobs and sighs;
I looked across the meadows near
To the towered church on the rise.
Overmuch cause had my look!
I pulled out pencil and book,
And drew a white chalk mound,
Outthrown on the sepulchred ground.

Why did I pencil that chalk?
It was fetched from the waiting grave,
And would return there soon,
Of one who had stilled his walk
And sought oblivion's cave.
He was to come on the morrow noon
And take a good rest in the bed so hewn.

He came, and there he is now, although
This was a wondrous while ago.
And the sun still dons a ruddy dye;
The weir still gurgles nigh;
The tower is dark on the sky.

COMPASSION

AN ODE

In Celebration of the Centenary of the Royal Society for the Prevention of Cruelty to Animals

I

BACKWARD among the dusky years
A lonesome lamp is seen arise,
Lit by a few fain pioneers
Before incredulous eyes.—
We read the legend that it lights:
"Wherefore beholds this land of historied rights
Mild creatures, despot-doomed, bewildered, plead
Their often hunger, thirst, pangs, prisonment,
In deep dumb gaze more eloquent
Than tongues of widest heed?"

II

What was faint-written, read in a breath
In that year—ten times ten away—

A larger louder conscience saith
More sturdily to-day.—
But still those innocents are thralls
To throbless hearts, near, far, that hear no calls
Of honour towards their too-dependent frail,
And from Columbia Cape to Ind we see
How helplessness breeds tyranny
In power above assail.

III

Cries still are heard in secret nooks,
Till hushed with gag or slit or thud;
And hideous dens whereon none looks
Are sprayed with needless blood.
But here, in battlings, patient, slow,
Much has been won—more, maybe, than we know—
And on we labour hopeful. "Ailinon!"
A mighty voice calls: "But may the good prevail!"
And "Blessed are the merciful!"
Calls a yet mightier one.

January 22, 1924.

"WHY SHE MOVED HOUSE"

(THE DOG MUSES)

WHY she moved house, without a word,
I cannot understand;
She'd mirrors, flowers, she'd book and bird,
And callers in a band.

And where she is she gets no sun,
No flowers, no book, no glass;
Of callers I am the only one,
And I but pause and pass.

TRAGEDIAN TO TRAGEDIENNE

SHALL I leave you behind me
When I play
In earnest what we've played in mock to-
day?

Why, yes; most surely shall I
Leave you behind
In yet full orbit, when my years unwind.

I may creep off in the night-time,
And none know
Till comes the morning, bringing news 'tis
so.

Will you then turn for a moment
White or red,
Recall those spells of ours; things done,
things said?

Aye, those adventurous doings
And those days
Of stress, when I'd the blame and you the
praise?

Still you will meet adventure—
None knows what—
Still you will go on changing: I shall not.

Still take a call at the mummings
Daily or nightly,
Yielding to custom, calmly, gloomily,
brightly.

Last, you will flag, and finish
Your masquings too:
Yes: end them: I not there to succour you.

THE LADY OF FOREBODINGS

"WHAT do you so regard, my lady,
Sitting beside me here?
Are there not days as clear
As this to come—ev'n shaped less shady?"
"O no," said she. "Come what delight
To you, by voice or pen,
To me will fall such day, such night,
Not, not again!"

The lamps above and round were fair,
The tables were aglee,
As if 'twould ever be
That we should smile and sit on there.
But yet she said, as though she must,
"Yes: it will soon be gone,
And all its dearness leave but dust
To muse upon."

THE BIRD-CATCHER'S BOY

"FATHER, I fear your trade:
Surely it's wrong!
Little birds limed and made
Captive life-long.

"Larks bruise and bleed in jail,
Trying to rise;
Every caged nightingale
Soon pines and dies."

"Don't be a dolt, my boy!
Birds must be caught;
My lot is such employ,
Yours to be taught.

"Soft shallow stuff as that
Out from your head!
Just learn your lessons pat,
Then off to bed."

Lightless, without a word
  Bedwise he fares;
Groping his way is heard
  Seek the dark stairs

Through the long passage, where
  Hang the caged choirs:
Harp-like his fingers there
  Sweep on the wires.

Next day, at dye of dawn,
  Freddy was missed:
Whither the boy had gone
  Nobody wist.

That week, the next one, whiled:
  No news of him:
Weeks up to months were piled:
  Hope dwindled dim.

Yet not a single night
  Locked they the door,
Waiting, heart-sick, to sight
  Freddy once more.

Hopping there long anon
  Still the birds hung:
Like those in Babylon
  Captive, they sung.

One wintry Christmastide
  Both lay awake;
All cheer within them dried,
  Each hour an ache.

Then some one seemed to flit
  Soft in below;
"Freddy's come!" Up they sit
  Faces aglow.

Thereat a groping touch
  Dragged on the wires
Lightly and softly—much
  As they were lyres;

"Just as it used to be
  When he came in,
Feeling in darkness the
  Stairway to win!"

Waiting a trice or two
  Yet, in the gloom,
Both parents pressed into
  Freddy's old room.

There on the empty bed
  White the moon shone,
As ever since they'd said,
  "Freddy is gone!"

That night at Durdle-Door *
Foundered a hoy,
And the tide washed ashore
One sailor boy.

November 21, 1912.

* Durdle-Door, a rock on the south coast.

A HURRIED MEETING

IT is August moonlight in the tall plantation,
Whose elms, by aged squirrels' footsteps worn,
Outscreen the noon, and eve, and morn.
On the facing slope a faint irradiation
From a mansion's marble front is borne,
Mute in its woodland wreathing.
Up here the night-jar whirrs forlorn,
And the trees seem to withhold their softest breathing.

To the moonshade slips a woman in muslin vesture:
Her naked neck the gossamer-web besmears,
And she sweeps it away with a hasty gesture.
Again it touches her forehead, her neck, her ears,

Her fingers, the backs of her hands.
She sweeps it away again
Impatiently, and then
She takes no notice; and listens, and sighs, and stands.

The night-hawk stops. A man shows in the obscure:
They meet, and passively kiss,
And he says: "Well, I've come quickly. About this—
Is it really so? You are sure?"
"I am sure. In February it will be.
That such a thing should come to me!
We should have known. We should have left off meeting.
Love is a terrible thing: a sweet allure
That ends in heart-outeating!"

"But what shall we do, my Love, and how?"
"You need not call me by that name now."
Then he more coldly: "What is your suggestion?"
"I've told my mother, and she sees a way,
Since of our marriage there can be no question.
We are crossing South—near about New Year's Day

The event will happen there.
It is the only thing that we can dare
To keep them unaware!"
"Well, you can marry me."
She shook her head. "No: that can never be.

" 'Twill be brought home as hers. She's forty-one,
When many a woman's bearing is not done,
And well might have a son.—
We should have left off specious self-deceiving:
I feared that such might come,
And knowledge struck me numb.
Love is a terrible thing: witching when first begun,
To end in grieving, grieving!"

And with one kiss again the couple parted:
Inferior clearly he; she haughty-hearted.
He watched her down the slope to return to her place,
The marble mansion of her ancient race,
And saw her brush the gossamers from her face
As she emerged from shade to the moonlight ray.

And when she had gone away
The night-jar seemed to imp, and say,
"You should have taken warning:
Love is a terrible thing: sweet for a space,
And then all mourning, mourning!"

DISCOURAGEMENT

TO see the Mother, naturing Nature, stand
All racked and wrung by her unfaithful lord,
Her hopes dismayed by his defiling hand,
Her passioned plans for bloom and beauty marred.

Where she would mint a perfect mould, an ill;
Where she would don divinest hues, a stain,
Over her purposed genial hour a chill,
Upon her charm of flawless flesh a blain:

Her loves dependent on a feature's trim,
A whole life's circumstance on hap of birth,
A soul's direction on a body's whim,
Eternal Heaven upon a day of Earth,
Is frost to flower of heroism and worth,
And fosterer of visions ghast and grim.

Westbourne Park Villas, 1863–7.
(From old MS.)

A LEAVING

KNOWING what it bore
I watched the rain-smitten
back of the car—
(Brown-curtained, such as the old ones
were)—
When it started forth for a journey afar
Into the sullen November air,
And passed the glistening laurels and round
the bend.

I have seen many gayer vehicles turn that
bend
In autumn, winter, and summer air,
Bearing for journeys near or afar
Many who now are not, but were,
But I don't forget that rain-smitten car,
Knowing what it bore!

SONG TO AN OLD BURDEN

THE feet have left the wormholed flooring,
That danced to the ancient air,
The fiddler, all-ignoring,
Sleeps by the gray-grassed 'cello player:
Shall I then foot around around around,
As once I footed there!

The voice is heard in the room no longer
That trilled, none sweetlier,
To gentle stops or stronger,
Where now the dust-draped cobwebs stir:
Shall I then sing again again again,
As once I sang with her!

The eyes that beamed out rapid brightness
Have longtime found their close,
The cheeks have wanned to whiteness
That used to sort with summer rose:
Shall I then joy anew anew anew,
As once I joyed in those!

278 SONG TO AN OLD BURDEN

O what's to me this tedious Maying,
    What's to me this June?
    O why should viols be playing
To catch and reel and rigadoon?
Shall I sing, dance around around around,
    When phantoms call the tune!

"WHY DO I?"

WHY do I go on doing these things?
Why not cease?
Is it that you are yet in this world of welterings
And unease,
And that, while so, mechanic repetitions please?

When shall I leave off doing these things?—
When I hear
You have dropped your dusty cloak and taken you wondrous wings
To another sphere,
Where no pain is: Then shall I hush this dinning gear.